Absalom, Absalom!

THE QUESTIONING OF FICTIONS

Twayne's Masterwork Studies
Robert Lecker, General Editor

Absalom, Absalom!

THE QUESTIONING OF FICTIONS

Robert Dale Parker

TWAYNE PUBLISHERS • BOSTON
A Division of G. K. Hall & Co.

Absalom, Absalom!: The Questioning of Fictions
Robert Dale Parker

Twayne's Masterwork Studies No. 76
Copyright 1991 by G. K. Hall and Co.
All rights reserved.
Published by Twayne Publishers
A division of G. K. Hall & Co.
70 Lincoln Street
Boston, Massachusetts 02111

Copyediting supervised by Barbara Sutton.
Book production by Janet Z. Reynolds.
Typeset by World Composition Services, Inc., Sterling, Virginia

10 9 8 7 6 5 4 3 2 1 (hc)
10 9 8 7 6 5 4 3 2 1 (pb)

The paper used in this publication meets the minimum requirements
of American National Standard for Information Sciences—Permanence
of Paper for Printed Library Materials, ANSI Z39.48-1984. ♾™

Printed and bound in the United States of America.

Library of Congress Cataloging-in-Publication Data

Parker, Robert Dale, 1953–
    Absalom, absalom! : the questioning of fictions / Robert Dale
Parker.
        p.   cm.—(Twayne's masterwork studies ; no. 76)
    Includes bibliographical references and index.
    ISBN 0-8057-8071-8.—ISBN 0-8057-8116-1 (pbk.)
    1. Faulkner, William, 1897–1962. Absalom, Absalom!   I. Title.
II. Series.
PS3511.A86A6763   1991
813'52—dc20   91-14216

Contents

Preface

This study of *Absalom, Absalom!* is aimed at the full range of readers, from thoughtful beginners to scholarly specialists in Faulkner studies. *Absalom, Absalom!* is forever telling readers already familiar with its tale that they need to start over and look again and forever pressing those who are discovering it for the first time to plunge into whirlwinds of speculation usually reserved for experts. Thus this book is organized so that people can read the novel two or three chapters at a time and then read the corresponding section of this book in the same way a student might attend a class after being asked to read each quarter or so of a long novel. In writing at once for beginners and old hands, I have found that, just as students can gain from encountering scholarly criticism, scholars need to take up issues (e.g., Sutpen's "wild niggers") that students often raise in the classroom but that are not the usual stuff of scholarship. For perhaps we have sometimes let scholarship wander too far from its secret sibling in pedagogy.

In recent decades literary criticism has seen some lively debate and change that has been slow to make its way into Faulkner studies and, to some extent, into the study of American literature in general. This book marks one effort in the movement to bring into Faulkner studies some of the concerns that those debates have prompted, and so it is written not only from an interest in Faulkner but also from an interest in a wide range of critical methods, including structuralism, poststructuralism, feminism, psychoanalysis, and cultural or social historicism, while recognizing and I hope taking advantage of the ways those methods are often at odds with each other. Perhaps my interest in competing perspectives is fitting in the study of an author and a novel dedicated to that principle. In any case, I have written in a language that should be accessible to those who know little or nothing of critical movements, for I believe that one obstacle to such inquiry is the elitist and obscurantist language it usually comes wrapped in.

In this study, then, I seek not simple answers but configurations of contending questions and answers. Much criticism of *Absalom, Absalom!* lays out too easily clear a perspective for a novel so diverse and self-contentious. Here I aim to clarify and read critically without contriving a simple, untroubled, or unanxious clarity. The most fitting readings of literature in general and *Absalom, Absalom!* in particular will seek out multiplicity, contradiction, and reverse implication, as in the half unbelievable last words of the novel: *"I don't hate it! I don't hate it!"*

Note on the References and Acknowledgments

All references to the novel, unless otherwise indicated, are to William Faulkner, *Absalom, Absalom!* (New York: Vintage, 1987). That edition is copyrighted 1986 and identified by the publishers as "the corrected text," edited by Noel Polk. Page numbers are given parenthetically.

It is a pleasure to thank the many friends and colleagues who encouraged this project, especially Mary Loeffelholz, who read a complete draft, and Bruce Michelson and Philip Graham, who each read portions of later drafts. The appendix evolved, through countless revisions, from R. W. B. Lewis's request that his students chart the novel's narrative structure. Although I started to think about this book before the series editor, Robert Lecker, proposed it, it might never have been written if he had not asked, and I am very grateful to him.

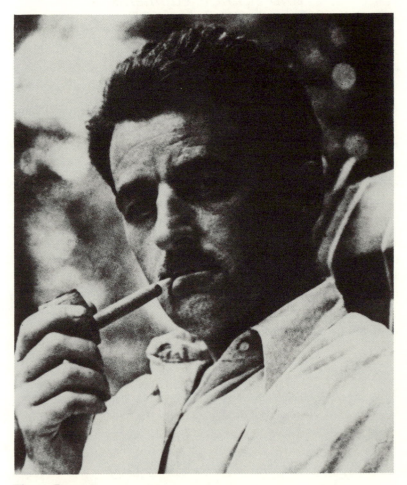

WILLIAM FAULKNER
Photograph by Marshall J. Smith, courtesy William Boozer Collection

Chronology:
William Faulkner's Life and Works

1897   William C. Falkner [*sic*] born in New Albany, Mississippi, to
            an artistic mother, who early on teaches Billy to read, and a
            bumbling father, who fails at one job after another. Billy also
            grows up amid legends of his swashbuckling great-grandfather,
            William C. Falkner, a Confederate colonel who helped restore
            white power in the 1870s and wrote a best-selling novel that
            romanticized Southern history. Colonel Sartoris, in Faulkner's
            fiction, is modeled partly on Colonel Falkner. Faulkner's grand-
            father on his mother's side had disappeared about 1888, with,
            as rumor had it, a beautiful "octoroon," suggestive of an epi-
            sode in *Absalom, Absalom!*

1898   Family moves to Ripley, Mississippi.

1902   Family moves to Oxford, Mississippi, county seat and site
            of the University of Mississippi. Caroline Barr, or "Mammie
            Callie," joins the family to help raise the Falkner boys, who
            soon grow close to her. She often entertains them with stories
            of slavery and reconstruction times. In Oxford, Bill grows up
            with Estelle Oldham. He often skips school, and he works in
            his father's livery stable, his grandfather's bank, and father's
            hardware store.

1907   Maternal grandmother, called Damuddy, dies (source for epi-
            sode in *The Sound and the Fury*).

1914   Begins friendship with Phil Stone, his major early sponsor.

1915   Quits eleventh grade, lives bohemian life.

1918   Estelle Oldham marries. Despondent, Faulkner leaves Oxford,
            bums around Yale University (where Phil Stone is law student),
            joins Canadian Royal Air Force. World War I ends while Faulk-
            ner still in training, leaving him deeply disappointed that he
            missed out on the fighting.

1918–1929   Fakes war injury, takes some college courses, works as college postmaster until fired for not delivering mail, continues bohemian life, mostly around Oxford, and also in New York, New Orleans (where he is befriended by Sherwood Anderson), and Europe.

1924   First book published, *The Marble Faun*, poetry.

1926   *Soldiers' Pay* published, first novel.

1927   *Mosquitoes* published.

1928   Cannot find publisher for his third novel, *Flags in the Dust*, the first of his Yoknapatawpha novels. Giving up on publishers—or so he later claims—starts to write the much more innovative *The Sound and the Fury* without publishing in mind.

1929   Estelle returns to Oxford from Honolulu and Shanghai, divorces her husband. She and Faulkner marry, bringing Faulkner two stepchildren; she tries to drown herself on their honeymoon. *Flags in the Dust* published in cut-down version as *Sartoris*. *The Sound and the Fury* published, Faulkner's first major novel.

1930   Buys run-down but stately antebellum mansion, restores it himself, and names it Rowan Oak. First published story, "A Rose for Emily." *As I Lay Dying* published.

1931   Daughter Alabama born, dies nine days later. *Sanctuary* published. First story collection published, *These Thirteen*.

1932   Desperate for money, Faulkner begins his intermittent career in Hollywood writing screenplays. Faulkner's father dies. *Light in August* published.

1933   Daughter Jill born. Faulkner learns to fly and buys airplane. Marriage with Estelle deteriorating.

1935   Younger brother Dean dies in plane crash while piloting plane Faulkner gave him; Faulkner supports his brother's wife and child. *Pylon* published.

1936   *Absalom, Absalom!* published.

1937   Health and stability deteriorating over the years, largely from alcoholism; repeatedly almost drinks himself to death and is institutionalized.

1938   Buys farm to breed mules. *The Unvanquished* published.

1939   *The Wild Palms* published.

1940   Caroline Barr dies. *The Hamlet* published, the first volume of the *Snopes* trilogy.

Chronology

Literary and
Historical Context

1

History and
Absalom, Absalom!

Faulkner began writing *Absalom, Absalom!,* with its grandiloquent and learned language and its passionate immersion in the past, in Oxford, Mississippi, in 1933 or 1934. Already the poorest state in the country, with the nation's worst schools, Mississippi was devastated by the Great Depression. Faulkner brought his manuscript to Hollywood several times, rising early to work at it before passing the days pounding out scripts for movies that he didn't believe in or care about. Hollywood must have seemed the opposite of Mississippi—Hollywood the tinseltown of showy wealth where everything was new and extravagant, feeding sybaritically off the hour and a half's dreamy, mass-produced and mass-marketed antidote to a world of misery. The range from Hollywood to small-town Mississippi makes it misleading to name one particular place or time in which *Absalom, Absalom!* was written. Moreover, though Faulkner wrote in the 1930s, he set his novel from the 1820s until 1910, and not only in Mississippi but also in New Orleans and Virginia, Harvard and Haiti. Even those places are hard to pin down, for Faulkner's Haiti doesn't make much historical sense, and he modeled his Harvard on Yale and on Oxford—Oxford, Mississippi, that is (site of the University of Mississippi). In *Absalom, Absalom!* the imagination seems at once to skip loose from the constraints of time and place and to insist that an immersion in a particular time and place can inspire a privileged intensity.

The sense of where and when Faulkner lived hangs over his writing, but it would be a mistake to think that his writing matters only or even primarily as a commentary on or an expression of the South. New England was central to Hawthorne, but people never say that they cannot understand *The Scarlet Letter* because they are not New Englanders, and it is part of our culture's condescension to the South to see its specialness as so prohibitive that people sometimes talk as if "The South" is the only lens through which we can see things Southern. Any number of times I have heard students and teachers say that they do not know how to read or teach Faulkner because they are not Southern—or that they do know because they are Southern. Many of those same people are Americans who study British literature, but they would smile with bemusement if anyone suggested that they must be British to understand Austen or Shakespeare or Dickens. To be of the South is in part also to be American, Western, white, black, or red, Christian or Jew, Methodist or Presbyterian, believer or skeptic, male or female, impoverished, comfortable, or wealthy, and so on—and for a writer, it is to be part of an international community of readers and writers that by definition takes one partly beyond one's own place and time, however much one brings one's own place and time along. Although these ideas are commonplaces, somehow such truisms fade when people take up Faulkner. There are many pasts and many places that *Absalom, Absalom!* both grows out of and contributes to: regional, national, and international; social, political, and literary; public and personal.

• • •

Faulkner's land of north Mississippi was home to the Chickasaw Indians in the early nineteenth century. They appear through much of

History and Absalom, Absalom!

Faulkner's fiction and turn up briefly in *Absalom, Absalom!*, where their only role is to surrender their land and silently disappear. In the 1820s and especially the early 1830s, the state and federal governments pressured most of the Chickasaws—as well as their Choctaw neighbors—into leaving Mississippi. When the fertile Indian hill country opened up for settlement, whites poured in, mostly poor folk from other Southern states. As a result, the 1830s were boom years in Mississippi—the state's first boom and so far its last. In 1830 the Mississippi economy, aside from a few counties along the river, did not depend on slaves, and Mississippi as a whole was probably little more committed to slavery than most Northern states. In the next decade that changed. To be sure, most farms remained small, with few slaves or none. But slavery, the plantation system, the cotton economy, and the state's population all grew enormously until by 1840 most Mississippians were black slaves (52 percent). When Mississippi seceded from the Union in 1861, there was little talk of issues like "states' rights," which Southern apologists would later say had motivated the Confederacy. The only issue that Mississippi secessionists raised was slavery.

The popular image of Mississippi as steeped in a long, genteel plantation heritage is therefore a myth. Until not many years before the Civil War, white settlers thought of themselves as Westerners, not Southerners. When war broke out in 1861, most whites worked small farms, and few plantations were more than a generation old. Cotton was the main cash crop but still amounted to a minority of agricultural production. Many whites opposed secession and war, not only farmers, who often had no slaves to defend, but also large plantation owners, who often held investments in the North and who understood the North's overwhelming economic and numeric superiority.

Contrary to myth, reconstruction was ably administered in Mississippi by honest and well-educated politicians, both black and white. In the mid-1870s, however, flagrantly racist whites won back control through intimidation and violence, and in the 1890s they took away the last remains of black political power through poll taxes and literacy

5

tests, administered unequally so as to keep out qualified blacks and let through illiterate whites. Sharecropping brought back slavery under another name and expanded it beyond blacks until by 1930 half the sharecroppers were white.

In Faulkner's youth, the dominating figure in Mississippi politics was the so-called White Chief, James K. Vardaman. On many issues Vardaman was passionately progressive, but his virulent racism overshadowed his reforms and galvanized poor whites, frightened of black economic competition, who might otherwise have found cause to align with blacks. Racial politics displaced economic politics, driving the already desperately suffering state yet deeper into poverty. Faulkner's grandfather, patriarch of the Falkner [*sic*] clan in the novelist's youth, was law partner to one of Vardaman's chief followers, and the Falkners aligned themselves with Vardaman and his political descendants. But even from his law partner—who later became governor—Faulkner's grandfather kept a distance, feeling himself the other man's social superior.

Meanwhile, while Mississippi remained agrarian and poor, the rest of the country grew wealthier, more industrial, and more urban. That brought America onto the international scene as a political and economic force. The Spanish-American War in 1898 marked the nation's emergence as a military power. The United States conquered Cuba and the Philippines and suddenly found itself one of the imperialist powers that so many Americans had long deplored. As white Americans conquered darker peoples across the waters, they saw an economic opportunity, and they also imagined some special duty of white rule, while at the same time Southern whites were consolidating their restoration to political and economic power over their black neighbors.

World War I provoked changes that, nevertheless, were still slow in coming. Black soldiers returned home with higher expectations, as some of Faulkner's fiction depicts. But social restrictions and the narrow economy left them almost nowhere to go unless they left for the North. By the time the stock market crashed in 1929, Mississippi was more dependent than ever on one crop, King Cotton. When cotton prices collapsed, Mississippi crumbled, encouraging more and more blacks to leave for the North. From 1860 to 1900, Mississippi was 60 percent black. By 1950, massive migration left the state hardly more than a third black, enabling whites to maintain political power even after blacks regained the vote.

In the 1930s, as Mississippi fell deeper into poverty, the rest of the world fared little better. Fascism and militarism, like Vardaman's racism, promised easy answers, winning the sway of millions. In Asia, World War II more or less began with Japan's attack on Manchuria in 1931, and people could see it coming in Europe long before Hitler attacked Poland in 1939. As Faulkner's frenzied style in *Absalom, Absalom!* suggests a sense of looming apocalypse in the American 1850s, just before the Civil War, so it also suggests a sense of Faulkner's contemporary world careening toward apocalypse.

Adding to and reflecting this sense of a world about to explode, a world in which progress could no longer be taken for granted, came the modernist revolution in art and science. Freud and Einstein described interior and exterior worlds that turned upside down what people had taken for granted, worlds that depend on unconscious motivation and nonlinear time. Those concepts encouraged novelists toward more intricate structures of narrative and character, as did the radical disruptions and reconstructions of modernist painting. Faulkner responded deeply to the most talked about modernist extravagances, from Cézanne and cubism to T. S. Eliot's "The Love Song of J. Alfred Prufrock" and *The Waste Land* and James Joyce's *Ulysses*. In such works, along with Marcel Proust's *Remembrance of Things Past,* he found prototypes for the alienation, the multiple narrative voices, and the inversions and disruptions of time and narrative that came to play so large a role in his novels. Meanwhile, the revival of *Moby-Dick* in the 1920s gave Faulkner an American model for many of the same experiments, as well as for *Absalom, Absalom!*'s almost Elizabethan opulence of language. Such difficulties of structure and language were part of an elite art that seems to have grown up partly in defiance of the more accessible and popular mass art produced to meet and indeed to create the taste of a rapidly growing audience. The elitism of modernist literature opened new channels of imagination, but socially they were narrower channels, in the sense that they would attract a smaller proportion of readers.

In American culture at large, Faulkner found his growing anguish over race relations, which would culminate in his novels of the 1940s. In literature, Harriet Beecher Stowe's *Uncle Tom's Cabin* and Mark Twain's *Adventures of Huckleberry Finn* and *Pudd'nhead Wilson* helped set the literary and cultural atmosphere for thinking about race relations, along with other novels—whether Faulkner read them or not—such as George Washington Cable's *The Grandissimes,* James Weldon Johnson's *The Autobiography of an Ex-Colored Man,* or Nella Larsen's *Quicksand* and *Passing.* Most of these works, like some of Faulkner's novels, explore the topic of mixed racial ancestry.

Absalom, Absalom! addresses older literatures as well. Its title alludes to the Old Testament story of David and his son Absalom (2 Sam. 13–19.4). Its language suggests the grandeur of Shakespeare's *Hamlet, Lear,* and *Othello.* And the novel evokes the familial and even national doom that hangs over Aeschylus's *Oresteia,* as well as over Faulkner's own earlier novel, *The Sound and the Fury.*

Indeed, the history in *Absalom, Absalom!* also comes out of Faulkner's personal and professional history. It is his sixth novel set in his imaginary Yoknapatawpha county—the county he sketched for the famous map at the back—and it is partly a sequel to *The Sound and the Fury.* While no one needs to read *The Sound and the Fury* to read *Absalom, Absalom!,* each novel can influence how we read the other. Still, though the two novels are related, they do not depend on each other, so that I will refer to *The Sound and the Fury* fairly often, but not in a way that my larger argument depends on. *The Sound and the Fury* focuses on the Compson family and its decay, including Quentin Compson's despair when his unmarried sister Caddy turns sexually active. Quentin wants to keep Caddy from leaving him. Partly for that reason, when she gets pregnant he explains to their father that he and Caddy have committed incest, but his father knows that Quentin is lying. Then, in June 1910, at the end of his first year at Harvard, Quentin drowns himself. Neither Quentin's sister nor his suicide gets mentioned in *Absalom, Absalom!* But readers who know about these concerns from the earlier novel may hear them echoing in the later work.

There is finally no absolute boundary between the history that surrounds and produces a work and the history that actually lies in the work and that the work itself contributes to making. We continue to reenvision the history in *Absalom, Absalom!* as our own history changes and leads us to read through changing perspectives, even as the characters in *Absalom, Absalom!* itself continually remake their own readings of their own history.

2

The Importance of
Absalom, Absalom!

Faulkner is the premier American modernist novelist and the most inventive experimenter in American modernist prose. In *Absalom, Absalom!*, the exuberant momentum of experiment, especially in the playful "either neither" passage near the novel's end, sometimes seems to carry Faulkner beyond the disruptions, distortions, and angst associated with modernism and into a delighted contemplation of his own modernist form. As the novel's storytelling begins to depend more and more conspicuously on the characters' actually telling the story to each other, they start to share in and reflect the novel's own exuberance about storytelling. In their thoughts about how to tell their stories, they begin to suggest a commentary on the art of storytelling itself. In that way, this supremely modernist novel begins also to anticipate the experiments of postmodernist fiction, sometimes called metafiction, or fiction about fiction, even if Faulkner never turns so arch as the American metafictionists who came to prominence in the 1960s and 1970s. Faulkner often seems to leave later American novelists looking back fearfully at his shadow, either imitating him or trying hard not to imitate him. Among metafiction writers, his influence shows more explicitly outside the United States, especially in Latin America and France, where unclassifiable, "either neither" writing, under whatever excuse for a label—the new novel or magical realism—has flowered the most lavishly. Thus *Absalom, Absalom!*, at the zenith of one movement in art and literature, seems to predict and prepare for another.

At the same time, *Absalom* makes so memorable an example of such movements partly because Faulkner never confines himself to representing the winds of any passing trend. *Absalom, Absalom!* is the greatest work of perhaps America's greatest novelist, one of that handful of American writers who so far have challenged readers the most pleasurably and provocatively. But the capacity to challenge does not reside literally between the covers of a book. It lies in the exchange of language and thought between the words on the page and the culturally constructed tastes and private energies of a diverse and ever evolving audience. In *Absalom*, the later characters' speculative uncertainty about the earlier characters sets them in a position like our own as we read and speculate about both sets of characters. That, in turn, provokes an awareness of how our shifting knowledge and judgments about the story in themselves become the story as much as the actions and judgments of the characters. Thus *Absalom* powerfully exposes the way that any story is an act of mind. For readers attuned to its challenge, *Absalom*'s bravura of language and form, its anguish over personal, regional, national, and more broadly social fears, and its celebration of story and talk through story and talk themselves all sound as deeply and fully as anything in American literature.

3

Critical Reception

By the time *Absalom, Absalom!* appeared, reviewers already approached Faulkner as one of America's great and controversial living novelists. Even so, most reviewers still felt mystified by his novels' intensity of emotion and style. Perhaps because of that intensity, Faulkner's books had not reached a large audience—except for *Sanctuary,* a succès de scandale that widened his reputation, though not always favorably. Many reviewers recognized *Absalom, Absalom!* as more ambitious than Faulkner's previous work, but some thought that his ambition led him astray. Faulkner's next two novels, much simpler than *Absalom, Absalom!,* received a heartier welcome, even getting him on the cover of *Time* magazine in 1939. Still, the acclaim for Faulkner did not add up to much in the popular imagination, by contrast, for example, with Hemingway, who cultivated fame in a way the more private Faulkner resisted. Meanwhile, amid the rapid stream of new Faulkner works, *Absalom, Absalom!* garnered no special attention. All Faulkner's books went out of print during World War II, and in America his reputation began to fade.

It did not fade in Europe, however. In occupied France simply to carry a book by Faulkner or Hemingway—both banned by the Nazis—became a sign of resistance, a badge of political and imaginative affiliation. Much of the keenest early writing on Faulkner came from France, and the French continue their special interest in him today. In Italy and Sweden the reaction was almost as enthusiastic. American readers started to return to Faulkner in the late 1940s. Malcolm Cowley's collection, *The Portable Faulkner,* came out in 1946, followed by a movie of *Intruder in the Dust* in 1949. When Swedish interest in Faulkner brought him the Nobel Prize in 1950, he at last found a large American audience.

At the same time, literary criticism in America was becoming a professional industry, and courses in American literature, which not long before seemed too contemporary and close to home for academic study, became routine. Those changes provided a means of distribution for Faulkner's novels at the same time that his work at last had a ready audience.

But not *Absalom, Absalom!,* which even Faulkner's most sympathetic critics often saw as a wild experiment gone awry. If one Faulkner novel pushed others aside, it was *The Sound and the Fury.* The opening or Benjy section of *The Sound and the Fury,* which provides so difficult an obstacle, is straightforward enough once you crack the code, so that its very difficulty becomes a handle that helps people grasp the book and hold it in memory. *Absalom, Absalom!* offers no such convenient path through its difficulties, no code ready to be cracked. Perhaps the critic who did the most to change perceptions of *Absalom, Absalom!* was Cleanth Brooks, whose many writings on the novel started to appear in the 1950s. No doubt, the greater seriousness that readers increasingly brought to Faulkner also encouraged more thoughtful attention to a work that might otherwise be dismissed as too demanding or eccentric. *Absalom*'s reputation steadily grew, until by the late 1970s a plurality of critics seemed to take it as Faulkner's greatest novel. It is no longer unusual to hear people refer to Faulkner as the "greatest" American novelist or to *Absalom, Absalom!* as the "greatest" American novel, even now that such concepts as "greatest" and "masterpiece" have come into question for making subjective consensus sound like objective and inherent fact.

As *Absalom, Absalom!* has drawn more interest, it has received an immense variety of critical responses, but a few patterns stand out. In some ways, it has been treated much as American literature has generally been treated since the 1950s under the influence of the so-called New Criticism, ushered in by, among others, Cleanth Brooks even before he wrote on Faulkner. The focus has been on interpreting the *text* and using it to represent the work of its individual author. American critics have shown less interest in *contexts,* in studying the text's role in a larger system or structure of literary genres like "the novel" itself or special kinds of novels, or studying its relation to the history of literary writing and reading, or studying its historical and social world. These other methods of criticism are more common outside the Anglo-American tradition, but are somewhat on the ascendancy now in Britain and America and have greatly influenced this study, even while it continues to focus on the text of Faulkner's novel.

Among the many issues critics have discussed we might note four areas of controversy. Some critics claim that the novel centers on the Compsons, while others insist that it centers on the Sutpens. Perhaps that debate derives from too ready an assumption that a novel must have a center in the first place and that it must center on a character, perhaps even a character that readers will identify with. But part of the complexity of *Absalom, Absalom!* comes from its defiance of such hackneyed expectations. Surely the novel is about both the Compsons and the Sutpens, and it serves no useful purpose to try to keep score and rank one family over the other.

Critics have also disagreed over whether *Absalom, Absalom!* should be considered by itself or in combination with *The Sound and the Fury*. Those who insist that it centers on the Compsons often insist that it must be read with *The Sound and the Fury*, since the Compsons appear in both novels and the Sutpens do not. But to insist on one side or the other of this disagreement is to construct a false dichotomy, as if the two novels must be either merged or isolated.

More thoughtfully, some critics have argued over whether Sutpen represents the old plantation South or whether he only wishes he could represent it. Opinions on the matter often have to do with how much critics like or dislike Sutpen and the old South. Faulkner himself seems to have encompassed the full range of allegiances without retreating from the contradictions they produced, leaving plenty of material for either side to offer as evidence.

Last, there has been much disagreement over whether and how things get explained at the novel's end, a controversy that the last chapter of this study will review closely.

• • •

The critical reception of *Absalom, Absalom!* extends beyond interpretive questions and into a rather interesting editorial history. Partly because *Absalom, Absalom!* is so unusual, its editors in 1936 reacted with confusion as well as admiration and made many changes in Faulkner's typescript. Thus the 1936 edition of *Absalom, Absalom!* was revised by hands other than Faulkner's. The editors have been accused of gross insensitivity, but perhaps it is too easy to make that charge, looking back from a time when the novel's reputation is secure. A few of their changes seem unexpectedly insightful, though they would have done better to leave things alone, and sometimes they made terrible mistakes. Thus the only text we have had for most of the time since the novel was published is what editors call a "corrupt" text.

Recently, however, Noel Polk has reedited *Absalom, Absalom!*, skillfully restoring the text as much as is practical to its state in Faulkner's typescript. Polk has been doing the same for Faulkner's other novels, and they have been appearing under the unfortunately presumptuous label "the corrected text." Polk's 1986 edition is about 30 pages longer than the earlier edition, and another 30 pages or so appear in considerably different form. He has also produced a facsimile of the typescript, which can help interested readers examine the materials for themselves.

In the Chronology and Genealogy at the back of the novel, however, Polk has violated his usually strict principles. Apparently, he assumes that Faulkner made some mistakes—a safe assumption for at least a few of the discrepancies—and therefore he has revised the Chronology and Genealogy to make them more consistent with the rest of the text. Readers who wish to see Faulkner's own version are therefore obliged to return to the 1936 edition.[1] Indeed, "mistakes" can be interesting, and in any case it seems too simple to write off all the irregularities as accidents.

Otherwise, Polk's edition is a superior text. It comes closer to what would have been Faulkner's so-called final intention (as they say in editors' lingo) if Faulkner had examined and compared all the surviving variants in the typescript and manuscript, as Polk has. But it seems that Faulkner never did examine and compare all the variants. And like most writers, he could change his mind or forget about things, despite his extraordinary meticulousness. In some instances, it seems that Faulkner never reached a single and final intention.

That has ramifications for the way we read the novel, because it sometimes leaves in question the very words we read—and even the punctuation, which this novel often flaunts. At a number of moments, then, we have no final authority to indicate Faulkner's preference. Since *Absalom* is, among other things, a book that sets final authorities in question, one cannot help thinking that Faulkner may have liked it that way.

A Reading

4

Without Rhyme or Reason or Shadow of Excuse: Chapters 1–3

Rosa's Voice

"Oh, I hold no brief for Ellen" (13), Miss Rosa Coldfield tells Quentin Compson in the first chapter of *Absalom, Absalom!* She must like those words, for she soon returns to them:

> No. I hold no more brief for Ellen than I do for myself. . . . I saw what had happened to Ellen, my sister. I saw her almost a recluse, watching those two doomed children growing up whom she was helpless to save. I saw the price which she had paid for that house and that pride; I saw the notes of hand on pride and contentment and peace and all to which she had put her signature when she walked into the church that night, begin to fall due in succession. I saw Judith's marriage forbidden without rhyme or reason or shadow of excuse; I saw Ellen die with only me, a child, to turn to and ask to protect her remaining child; I saw Henry repudiate his home and birthright and then return and practically fling the bloody corpse of his sister's sweetheart at the hem of her wedding gown; I saw that man return—the evil's source and head which had outlasted all its victims—who had created two children not only to destroy one

another and his own line, but my line as well, yet I agreed to marry him.

   No. I hold no brief for myself. I don't plead. (17–18)

Rosa's voice rules over the beginning of *Absalom, Absalom!* so grandiosely that we can hardly tell how to respond. "Her voice would not cease, it would just vanish" (4), as if its influence hovers over the more timidly reflective Quentin even when she slows for an orator's dramatic pause. In her cramped room, with Quentin as her awkward audience of one, Rosa's feverish insistence seems like misplaced melodrama. Yet there is something mesmerizing in her "dim coffin-smelling gloom sweet and oversweet with the twice-bloomed wistaria against the outer wall by the savage quiet September sun" (4). The spell comes partly from how everything here turns two ways: coffin-smelling and sweet, sweet and oversweet, twice-bloomed, savage and quiet, dimly gloomy and sunny.

   Self-absorbed, a little bored, a little resentful and irritated, and yet (since everything turns two ways) fascinated too, Quentin cannot understand that doubleness. The sympathy Quentin attracts as heir to the romantic tradition of youthful and heroic alienation can lead us to respond to Rosa with some of his bewildered impatience. Like Quentin, we suddenly find ourselves the passive victims of Rosa's harangue, wondering, as he wonders (10), why we are there at all. But even while Faulkner steers us to Quentin's view of Rosa, he also allows us to see Quentin with skepticism. If we thus step aside from Quentin's cynicism, we can see Rosa more sympathetically. For Rosa's doubleness makes her more complicated and less the stereotype of an old maid than the self-absorbed Quentin can understand.

   On the one hand, Quentin's surroundings—and Faulkner's, and still to a considerable extent our own—set judgment against Rosa. She is old and alone in a culture that defines women's value by their familial or sexual relation to others rather than by their urge to quest for themselves. Indeed, it is easier to say what the novel begins with if we concentrate, as readers usually have, on the familiar anguishing young man. But it also begins with the less familiar sound of Rosa Coldfield's keen and passionate intelligence. Rosa's voice differs from the condescending and, in some sense, authorial voice of the first two paragraphs, and from the voice we hear in Quentin's thoughts or in his father's hodgepodge of erudition and folksy yarn-spinning in chapters 2 and 3. Her voice is incantatory, orotund and oratorical with its stump speaker's repetitive pattern (technically known as *anaphora*), eight times beginning a statement by insisting on and detailing what she *saw*, and nesting even that series of eight within a similarly self-dramatized opening exclamation of "No. I hold no brief"—first "for Ellen," and then "no more for Ellen than I do for myself," and then at last completing the claim by saying that she holds "no brief for myself."

Such forceful rhetoric projects a voice of intelligence and power. In comparison, the female characters in Faulkner's earlier novels are rarely so self-aware, and rarely does he see in them a sympathetic and articulate intelligence, or tell the story through their perceptions and ruminations. In the novels before *Absalom, Absalom!*, he continues the familiar literary practice of imagining women through the eyes of men. It is sometimes thought that perspective or point of view is power. That is, that when writers portray events through the eyes of a particular character, they give that character power and perhaps attribute power to that *kind* of character, to a gender, class, age, or temperament. If so, then Faulkner's focus on Rosa and on the story as seen through Rosa's perspective could suggest a major change for him.

But Faulkner, as we have started to see, works in two directions. He diminishes Rosa's power and intelligence by making her seem cranky and remote, yet he gives her an intensity and intellectual command that neither Quentin nor the novel's readers can comfortably push aside. And so he constructs an implicit commentary on the urge to deny or turn away from power when it comes in Rosa's elderly feminine and socially disconnected form. He at once participates in and disparages the feeling of being put upon by Rosa's off-key etiquette and unauthorized power. On the one hand, he portrays Rosa's authority in a form that mocks those who, like Quentin, would evade noticing it. On the other hand, he apparently needs, like Quentin, to protect against her command by dressing her in forms he is accustomed to condescend to. He imagines a woman of great verbal and oratorical power, whose first poems he calls her "first folio" (8) as if to associate her—again half mockingly—with the first folio of Shakespeare. And surely verbal power is central to Faulkner's own imagination in this novel. But he also makes her seem asexual and alone, without any of the things that traditionally ascribe value to a woman's life, without husband, children, or family, without even—Faulkner lets us know from the first sentence—a commonsensical notion of housekeeping. Lost in the past, she seems helpless next to Quentin's feeble (it turns out) but still obligatory young man's sense of his emerging self as the bearer of a burgeoning future. The very act of Rosa's summoning Quentin to help her reaffirms her dependence. It might seem then that Faulkner can afford to empower Rosa (or, say, Aunt Jenny Du Pre in *Flags in the Dust* and *Sanctuary,* or Granny Millard in *The Unvanquished*) because she no longer counts in the ways—mostly erotic—that women characters in other books seem to count most to him. It may seem, in other words, that in Faulkner's fiction old women are safe women, and so only old women can be canny and authoritative women.

Still, Faulkner imagines Rosa with more enthusiasm than his defensive condescension might suggest. Poignantly, he seems caught between dismissing Rosa more or less as demanded by the traditional condescensions of Faulkner's own social world, and lingering over her with a more personal enthusiasm, encouraged not only by ordinary feeling for his characters, but probably also by admiration for his hard-driving mother and his beloved, quick-witted Aunt Bama. Regardless where it comes from, the enthusiasm seems unmistakable. Rosa's voice gives *Absalom, Absalom!* so much of its sumptuous eloquence that, despite her lonely pitifulness, Rosa comes close to something like Faulkner's own fierce ideal, to the voice of *Absalom, Absalom!* itself. Critics often link Quentin's yearnings to Faulkner's own youthful angst. But Rosa is every bit as close as Quentin to Faulkner's novel-writing, language-fashioning self. In a sense Rosa is Quentin grown up, with the same Southern sense of doom and would-be intellectual's memories of agonized adolescence that Quentin seems never able to escape, yet matured and assertive as Quentin will never be.

Moreover, as Faulkner conceives her, Rosa undermines and complicates the urge to patronize her that he both counts on and satirizes, for she admits her failure. In her flamboyant anaphora, she insists that she holds "no brief for myself." The flamboyance and the disclaimer are delightfully at odds: in masterful language, Rosa disavows mastery. With dramatically intensifying syntactical complexity, including (in this case) rhyme ("oh" and "no," "more" and "for") and assonance picking up the sound of the rhyme ("Oh, I hold no. . . . No. I hold no . . . ."), Rosa rules her oratorical realm. Her rolling off sentence after sentence with "I saw" suggests an almost visionary quality, as with each incantatory repetition she adds to her gradually accumulating resonance of power by insisting that she saw not just random things but rather, each time, someone else's loss. The contrast between her losses and the authority she proclaims them with makes it almost possible, amid her obscure references to things not yet explained, to overlook that she likens herself to the losers: she holds no more brief for herself than she does for them. Yet her forceful language establishes a difference from them that makes her unafraid to proclaim her failure with theirs. She figures her insistence in legal and economic or debtors' language (brief, plead, notes of hand, price), ritualizing her history of flouted desire in a language of controlled exchange that allows her to recover rhetorically the losses that she once could see and feel but not speak.

Quentin and his father see Rosa's loss of control but not her recovery. Her verbal onslaught doesn't interest Quentin much. Instead of listening, he lets his thoughts wander to his own memories of the legend she describes (10–11). He tries to deny her power by seeing her as no more than a medium for her story, as if she were as merely incidental—even to her own story—as he feels right then sitting awkwardly before her. "If he threw her over," Quentin says to his father at the beginning of chapter 3, "I wouldn't think she would want to tell anybody about it." But Rosa never says that Sutpen threw her over; nor is there any sign that local legend says he did. Quentin unthinkingly assimilates what he doesn't know of Rosa's story into a more general male mythology: the tale of the jilted woman, the Miss Havisham figure from Dickens's *Great Expectations* that Rosa indeed resembles and that Faulkner had already studied in "A Rose for Emily." It can seem to reassure some men to see women as rejected rather than rejecting. Quentin, at least, is too self-involved to care about Rosa. From the perspective he takes for granted, she seems too solitary and old, too femininely peripheral to his life and even to the central events of her own life. Yet, condescend to Rosa as he might, Quentin still finds it difficult to reconcile his vague assumptions of her insignificance with his immediate sense of her authority in the cramped hot airless room, and that difficulty helps account for the uneasiness just beneath his young gentleman's ritual of laconic modesty and respectful manners, of "Yessum" and "Nome."

Nor is Rosa herself free from the ideology that makes Quentin condescend to her. For the assumptions of that ideology are unconscious and cultural rather than chosen and personal. And so her figurative language of control, of finance and law, itself figures another language of being controlled, of fate. She talks of doomed children and a helpless mother, not of the notes of hand themselves so much as of their inevitable and relentless falling due. Her rhetorical confidence jars with her inability to explain, her sense that it all happened "without rhyme or reason or shadow of excuse." The language of control thus seems not only a mark of her rhetorical authority but also a grasping defense against her *loss* of control. If we fail, it can soothe us to think that *we* didn't cause the failure, *fate* did. And the oppressive feel of supposed fate closing down on family is one of Faulkner's characteristic subjects. The Rosa who controls is therefore both product and cause of the Rosa who cannot control. In fact, despite her incantatory insistence, it turns out that much of what Rosa tells Quentin she saw, she never did see.

Without Rhyme or Reason or Shadow of Excuse

She may say "I saw Judith's marriage forbidden without rhyme or reason or shadow of excuse," and for the first chapter readers have little more than Rosa's absolute befuddlement to serve as explanation, a bewildering predicament as we muddle through the maze of syntax and through events and characters that, as Faulkner puts it, "abrupt" (4) into the narrative without introduction. But even that early in the book we have at least one hint beyond Rosa's insistence that there is no explanation, because for Rosa to say that she "saw" it does not mean that it was so. It turns out that Rosa did not *see* Judith's marriage forbidden without rhyme, reason, or excuse; she simply heard that people *supposed* it was forbidden, and she never heard any reason why. For all she knows, it never was forbidden. Similarly, she never saw Henry repudiate home and birthright. Nor did she see him return or "practically fling" Bon's corpse at Judith. In a way, then, Rosa sees little, but is obsessed with her vision.

Indeed, her story centers on others, on the Sutpens. She spends her youth as a watcher rather than a participant—as Quentin in both this novel and *The Sound and the Fury* watches rather than participates—and spends her long adulthood continuing to watch through the retrospect of obsessive memory. It seems as if she has frozen emotionally on the man she agreed to marry and yet somehow, like Dickens's Miss Havisham, did not marry—the "long-dead object of her impotent yet indomitable frustration" (4). As Miss Havisham spends the rest of her life in her white wedding gown, Rosa has worn her "eternal black . . . for forty-three years," ever since the deaths of her sister, her father, and her marriage-to-be—any of which might be the event she mourns (3). The external narrator, who provides the not very sympathetic tone of words like "impotent" and "frustration" as well as the grudging admiration of a word like "indomitable," shadows Rosa's opening vision of Sutpen with a mocking parenthetical aside—"(man-horse-demon)"—that all but smirks at her fascinated image of his manly, animal, satanic potency (4). Like Miss Havisham, Rosa locks her life on the marriage she almost but never made.

It might trouble us that for Rosa (and perhaps Faulkner), the women of this novel, including herself, hold interest only through their relation to marriage and men. Just as the external narrator defines Rosa through her fixation on a thwarted marriage, so Rosa defines Judith Sutpen solely in relation to her father and *her* thwarted marriage, identifying Judith as the "daughter who was already the same as a widow without ever having been a bride and was, three years later, to be a widow sure enough without having been anything at all" (13–14). For Rosa, in a strikingly pathetic phrase, never to have been married is never to have been anything at all. So that when she defines her relation to the novel's plot by insisting, as she puts it, that " 'I hold no more brief for Ellen than I do for myself,' " she defines both her sister and herself by their willingness—to her indefensible—to marry Sutpen the ogre. Their acquiescence in the ogre's desire is not, for her, simply a major incident in their lives. It is the single incident that defines their lives, exactly as she sees the prevention of Judith's marriage as the defining fact of Judith's life. She cannot step back to contemplate her reliance on such definitions; she can only abide by them. They are part of the ideology around and within her that she unconsciously subscribes to. Even so, she senses that something is peculiar.

She wonders why she would agree to a marriage that she "saw" destroy her sister and her sister's children, but every answer she can think of, she disavows. "I dont plead youth," she says. "I dont plead propinquity. . . . I dont plead material necessity . . . though I defy anyone to blame me. . . . And most of all, I do not plead myself," by which she means that she doesn't "plead" the excuse of adolescent lust, or, in her euphemism, of a "young woman emerging" (18). She can say only what she does *not* plead, for she has no notion of what she does plead. To Rosa, in the forty-third year of her bewilderment, even what is most central, the very thing that defines Ellen, Judith, and Rosa herself, is without rhyme, reason, or shadow of excuse. And so she moves on from her list of negatives, her list of what she does not plead, and rather than saying what she does plead she simply circles back—in the looping, digressive manner of a book shaped out of people's talking—to where she began. She leaves the unexplainable story of her submission to Sutpen's proposal and drifts back to the tale of its prototype in Ellen's submission a generation before. She sees nothing in her life or her sister's or Judith's life that gains any significance at all apart from how it anticipates or reacts to their disastrous or thwarted marriages.

We might therefore challenge or complicate the impulse to criticize the supposedly stark grid of gender differentiation in some of Faulkner's earlier work, including *The Sound and the Fury* and *As I Lay Dying*. Faulkner focuses those novels, quite unlike the beginning of *Absalom*, mostly through the eyes of male characters preoccupied or even obsessed with a female character, and hardly ever through the eyes of the female character who is the object of male obsession. That can imply that power is masculine and that the feminine is secondary, defined by a subservience to erotic masculine imagination and observation. It can take the subject of power as masculine and the object of power as feminine (using *subject* and *object* according to the analogy between the grammar of a sentence and the structure or, in effect, grammar of a narrative). The masculine can thus seem the domain of action and the feminine the domain of passivity, so much so that Faulkner's decision to give Rosa voice and to make her obsessed with imagining and observing a man, Thomas Sutpen, can seem like a critical revision of his earlier pattern.

But we have seen how Rosa's circumstances are more complicated than that notion of men as active and women as passive would imply. She is at once active as a speaker and passive as a watcher of other people's actions. She passively subscribes to defining women by their relation to men and marriage, yet she spends her life endlessly perplexed at her own capitulation to the memory of a man and her wish to marry him. Even in *The Sound and the Fury* and *As I Lay Dying* the structural relation between gender and narrative role disperses across a more diffuse grid than readers sometimes suspect, because the male characters do not in every way assume an active role in relation to passively feminine objects. In those novels, the masculine voices are also voices of failure, of inconsequence and impotence awestruck before the freedom of active, feminine power and of feminine erotic will rather than erotic subservience. The women do, and the men, unable to do, are confined to watch and reflect upon what the women do.

For Faulkner's fiction, then (and not only for Faulkner's), the familiar oppositions of active and passive, subject and object, impose an artificial dichotomy on a complicated, anguished relation. Watched characters, passive in the narrative (the telling of the tale) in that they hardly speak, are watched for their action in the plot (the tale that is told). And watching characters, active in the narrative, can otherwise sit passively apart from the action. And so, simply to make a female character speak is not to give her a voice; it depends on what she says. When Rosa speaks, she reproduces the patronizing ideology that defines her and other women solely through their relation to men. In that sense, she unwittingly ventriloquizes a larger cultural voice. But at the same time, in her "indomitable" bewilderment, her active resentment of her own passivity, she starts to tug at a dangling thread, starts to tease out an implied contradiction in the larger ideology around her. She feels, rather than interprets, that she can be at once both passive and active. Thus to describe Rosa and her role in *Absalom, Absalom!* demands a more complicated language than the familiar rubrics that might lead us simply to call her either an oppressed, victimized woman or a heroically independent, rebellious woman. Such terms often come up in the classroom and—sometimes more guardedly—in scholarly criticism, whether for Rosa or for women characters in other novels by Faulkner or other writers. We should resist the common impulse to dismiss Rosa or Quentin because they are secondary to the plot action—a formula that often works to the disadvantage of women characters and even women writers, who often prefer more interior plots—just as we should resist the opposite and equally common impulse to dismiss Sutpen because he is secondary to the storytelling. Different figures command different interests, and each gives us more of that difference from ourselves that is part of what we read novels for in the first place.

THE PLOT

Readers may well find themselves struggling not only to assimilate the novel's startlingly intense opening character, but also simply to pick out the plot. Surprisingly, for so complicated a book, the gnarled prose keeps curling up into microcosms, into parts that spell out and represent the whole. Early on, as Rosa tells Quentin her story, he drifts off into his own thoughts, with their quiet privacy and intensity heightened by Faulkner's switch to italics. He reviews for himself (5–6)—and, conveniently, for readers—the story already familiar to him (9, 34) as local legend: how Thomas Sutpen appeared suddenly from nowhere, violently tore a plantation from the wilderness, married Rosa's sister Ellen, and begot a son and daughter. Then suddenly the summary turns vague: *"they destroyed him or something or he destroyed them or something."*

Quentin feels as mystified as readers probably feel. As Faulkner soon puts it in another microcosm (dozens of these microcosms crop up through the novel, far too many to point out), "Quentin seemed to see them, the four of them arranged into the conventional family group of the period, . . . a picture, a group which even to Quentin had a quality strange, contradictory and bizarre; not quite comprehensible, not (even to twenty) quite right" (12). Quentin is in our position, trying to make sense of or interpret a tiny skein of facts that seems flimsily out of proportion to all that Rosa so melodramatically makes of them. As so often in Faulkner's novels, we get the effect before the cause, and the urge to uncover the cause impels the plot and suspense. Even Rosa, in the passage we began with, summarizes the story when, item by item, she chants what she "saw": her sister Ellen inexplicably married Thomas Sutpen and lived almost as a recluse while their two children, Henry and Judith, grew up; Sutpen forbade Judith's marriage for—so far as Rosa can see—no reason. Ellen died, and later Henry repudiated his inheritance and killed his sister's fiancé. Then Rosa, as inexplicably as her sister, agreed to marry Sutpen even though she blames him as the source of all the tragedy, and even though we have heard from the first page—which refers to him as her "nothusband"—that they never went through with the marriage. Rosa's explanation (if we can call it that), which we will make a touchstone for interpreting Rosa and comparing her view to other characters' views, is thus that she has no explanation: without rhyme or reason or shadow of excuse.

Quentin has hardly any more of a clue than Rosa, so that Faulkner's tendency to spell out the plot in little microcosms starts to take on ironic resonance, as if he throws out the information partly to tease us with our failure to understand it. In one sense that failure troubles Quentin even more than it might trouble readers, because, having grown up with the story, Quentin feels he should understand it. On the other hand, because he has grown up with it, Quentin has no need to explain things systematically as he reviews them in his mind. And that partly accounts for the confusion readers find, since Faulkner tells much of the first chapter through Quentin's thoughts, and Quentin has no need to explain to himself what he already knows. Thus, as in the so-called stream-of-consciousness narrative that Faulkner learned from Joyce's *Ulysses* and then worked his own variations on in *The Sound and the Fury* and *As I Lay Dying,* we get a clear picture of Quentin's *process* of thought at the sacrifice of a clear history of the matters he thinks about. Faulkner could, one supposes, tell the story more forthrightly, but then he would lose the feeling of immersion in the minds of Quentin and Rosa.

As we have noted, Quentin and Rosa have much in common. The opening description of Rosa, beginning with the time of day in her "dim hot airless room with the blinds all closed," with the sun slanting through the lattices and a rustle of sparrows outside the window, recalls the opening pages of Quentin's section in *The Sound and the Fury,* underlining the analogy between Rosa and Quentin. If the opening description also suggests an analogy between character and setting, between the dim airless room and the woman it belongs to, between Rosa's emotions and her little legs that "hung straight and rigid as if she had iron shinbones and ankles, clear of the floor with that air of impotent and static rage like children's feet," then it can help to note again the novel's double-sidedness. Because our culture tends to look down at old, especially never-married women, many readers note such analogies without also noting the things that undermine them, such as the twice-blooming wistaria outside the window of this woman named for a flower, or how, at the dramatic end of the novel's first paragraph, Rosa has the power, despite 43 years of impotence and stasis, to call up the mesmerizing vision of Sutpen. Quentin is similarly double-sided. On the one hand, he doesn't even know why he is there: "But why tell me about it?" (10; see also 8) he asks his father. Yet he feels there must be something special about him that has made Miss Rosa Coldfield, whom he barely even knows, summon him for her tirade.

His father answers with a long, tenuous explanation (10–11) that introduces the indulgences of Mr. Compson—here in his first words—as much as it answers the question. Nevertheless, by the time he concludes, his answer is astonishing. Maybe, he says, the vast Sutpen tragedy, fading almost two generations into the past, is somehow *Quentin's* fault, an answer not calculated to comfort his already anxious son. If Quentin has felt, or wanted to feel, as distant from Rosa as readers at first are apt to feel, then his father's labored explanation insists that Rosa's story is somehow also Quentin's story and, by implication, that the seemingly distant past is also the story of us all. Or is that only what Mr. Compson, for motives of his own, would like Quentin to think? After all, Mr. Compson oddly skips over his own role in passing guilt unto the next generation. It is hard to tell about Mr. Compson, especially in this first chapter where he plays only a minor, parenthetical role. In chapters 2 and 3 he steps onto the stage more largely, but before we turn to those chapters it may help to pause and take account of the novel's narrative structure, as we will do periodically, for it grows steadily more intricate.

Already in the first chapter the narrative splits in two: characters in the twentieth century (Rosa Coldfield, Quentin Compson, and his father, referred to as "Mr" Compson) agonize over a story about characters in the nineteenth century (the Sutpens—Thomas, Rosa's sister Ellen, and their children Henry and Judith). The narrative splits in other ways as well, moving across different systems of narrative time and different levels of interior reflection or speculative intensity. In *The Sound and the Fury*, a change to italics often indicates a change in time. As Faulkner tried to explain to his friend and literary agent, Ben Wasson, who without Faulkner's permission took the italics out of *The Sound and the Fury*, the italics themselves (which Faulkner painstakingly restored after Wasson removed them) do not refer to any particular time.[1] But the shift *between* italics and roman refers to a shift between any of many different times.

In *Absalom, Absalom!* the structural principle is the same, even though the changes in typeface signify abstract shifts in consciousness rather than, as in *The Sound and the Fury*, shifts between particular times in the characters' memories. Faulkner sometimes slips into italics to suggest a leap in the intensity of Quentin's reflection (as on 5–6, 8, 12) without a change in time. Still, not all deep reflectiveness comes italicized. Rather than attributing some inherent meaning to the fact of italics itself, Faulkner uses the shift *between* italic and roman type to indicate a shift in the kind of thought his language represents, but not necessarily a shift of the same sort in each instance.

In *Absalom*, the shifts between times hold to a more conventional typography and come nowhere near as rapidly as in *The Sound and the Fury*. But already in the first chapters they can seem oddly complicated—and later they will grow far more mysterious than in *The Sound and the Fury*. From the first sentence, Faulkner signals the novel's interest in time. He then takes a relatively conventional turn, backing up to review things from earlier in the day that lead up to the book's opening event (7). But soon he leaps forward to interrupt himself and say that "it would be three hours yet before he [Quentin] would learn why she had sent for him" (9), and then he inserts a two-paragraph digression, in parentheses, giving a conversation later that day between Quentin and his father as they try to interpret the very episode that Faulkner has them interrupt.

Each chapter is thus set in at least two different times, which I will call a time present and a time past (see the appendix). In the first three chapters, the time present begins "a little after two oclock" on a "long still hot weary dead September afternoon" (3) and continues pretty straightforwardly into that evening. The time past is more complicated, though simple compared to later in the novel. The times past of chapters 2 (June 1833 to June 1838) and 3 (1855 to 1866) are embedded in the larger time past of chapter 1 (June 1833 to 1866), which suggests that the first chapter, logically enough, introduces the story with an overview, preparing for the next two chapters to return to the same material in more detail. Simple as that seems, it can help us sort out and acclimatize to the novel's intricate structure. If we see chapter 1 as an introduction or overture, then it can similarly help to think of chapter 2 as "The Mysterious Arrival and Courtship of Thomas Sutpen" and of chapter 3 as "The Childhood of Rosa Coldfield," although both those titles, especially chapter 3, demand the ungainly supplement "as told, imagined, and interpreted by Mr. Compson."

Mr. Compson's Voice

How does Mr. Compson know? His father, General Compson, told him things that he saw or heard around town or learned directly from Thomas Sutpen, and his mother reported things that she heard, sometimes from Ellen Sutpen. Mr. Compson has also heard a great deal from the talk and legend of small-town lore.

In chapter 2, as Mr. Compson's somewhat more variable voice takes over from Rosa, he turns for a stretch to a comic and almost folksy sound: "They just waited while reports and rumors came back to town of how he and his now somewhat tamed negroes had installed the windows and doors and the spits and pots in the kitchen and the crystal chandeliers in the parlors and the furniture and the curtains and the rugs; it was that same Akers who had blundered onto the mudcouched negro five years ago [40] who came, a little wild-eyed and considerably slack-mouthed, into the Holston House bar one evening and said, 'Boys, this time he stole the whole durned steamboat!' " (51).

This is the tall tale, oral style of humor that Mark Twain thrived on and that Faulkner pursues at length elsewhere. Here, it is an especially communal storytelling; Mr. Compson and the town have pieced together his tale like a patchwork quilt of scraps collected across the social spectrum—from discrete and respectable General Compson to gullible riffraff like the apocryphal Akers. On the other hand, social humor though it is, it also tells an in-joke for the reader—or writer—of Faulkner's fiction, since Faulkner had already published a story ("Red Leaves") in which someone really does steal a whole steamboat, rolling it improbably over hill and dale all the way from the Mississippi River to Yoknapatawpha. In moments like this, Mr. Compson's words do not reflect his own personality. They could almost come from any other garrulous raconteur who can stir up the town's gossip and ladle it out for Quentin.

Then, in chapter 3, Faulkner drops the quotation marks from Mr. Compson's storytelling. Does this change give the narrative more authority, because it makes it seem as if the story now comes from a more or less omniscient perspective? Or does it give the narrative *less* authority, because the quirk of shifting typography indicates a self-consciousness that casts suspicion on Faulkner's protracted reliance upon one self-indulgent perspective? Or might it give the narrative a *false* authority, an impression of assurance that lulls us away from doubts that later circumstances might reawaken? It seems to raise several possibilities at once, thus dramatizing the possibility of competing authorities, and of competing possibilities *for* authority.

And that leaves us wondering about Mr. Compson's voice and perspective. Does he put his own stamp on the story he tells, and to the extent he does, how should that shape the way we understand his story? On a second reading, most readers pick out Mr. Compson's style and see it as coloring his tale, and some do on a first reading, especially if they already know how he appears in *The Sound and the Fury* or its sneering Appendix, written a decade after *Absalom* and so, perhaps, partly influenced by *Absalom*.

When the narrative switches from an exterior, more or less authorial voice to the particular voice of Mr. Compson (49), it gives us a place to measure Mr. Compson's distinctiveness. The change is anything but abrupt; some readers don't even notice it. Indeed, in the manuscript, the change to Mr. Compson's narration comes later than in Faulkner's final version (at what is now p. 56, "It was in June . . .").[2] But from the start, Mr. Compson says things that personalize his storytelling and differentiate it from the chapter's earlier, external narrative. In the manuscript, none of his more personal phrasings appears in the passage that the manuscript puts in an exterior voice but that the finished novel puts in Mr. Compson's voice (49–56). In the finished novel, Mr. Compson addresses Quentin personally, referring repeatedly to what "your Grandfather said," versus the earlier, external narrator's more distanced reliance on the third-person (e.g., 47). And he lingers over his thoughts in the first person: "But I dont think so. That is, I think it was a little more involved" (50). With a witty, ironical embroidery that will start to seem characteristic, Mr. Compson compares Sutpen's "florid, swaggering gesture" to "John L. Sullivan having taught himself painfully and tediously to do the schottische" (52–53). And almost as soon as he takes over in his own voice, he moves into talk of Sutpen's "wild niggers" (50).

Some readers feel ill at ease about such talk, which they don't expect from a famous, supposedly "great" work, especially in the twentieth century. But the expression "wild niggers" and the comedy of the supposedly wild slaves' exile from their homeland and language do not come simply from Faulkner. They come from the town whose attitudes Faulkner and his characters report. To be sure, the troubling comedy of Sutpen's slaves turns up first in the authorial voice, near the beginning of the novel when Rosa's words summon the ghost of Sutpen: "Out of quiet thunderclap he would abrupt (man-horse-demon) upon a scene peaceful and decorous as a schoolprize water color, faint sulphur-reek still in hair clothes and beard, with grouped behind him his band of wild niggers like beasts half tamed to walk upright like men, in attitudes wild and reposed" (4–5). These are the words of the exterior narrative voice, and not of Rosa. Still—though it is hard to realize early in the novel, especially for first-time readers—these thoughts come through the perspective of Rosa. It is not unusual for writers to render their characters' thoughts and some of their words indirectly, rather than presenting those thoughts word for word. Such *free indirect discourse,* or *style indirect libre,* as critics sometimes call it, allows a playful movement in and out of a character's mind and pressures readers to work at defining their sense of character and narrator, to ask, as we now are asking, Does such a language and perspective fit Rosa? Does such a language and perspective fit the narrator? What else do we see in Rosa or the narrator to help us recognize and wonder about their patterns of perception and ideology?

Nowhere in *Absalom, Absalom!,* and nowhere, I believe, after Faulkner's early work does he use, in the novelist's or story writer's voice, the word *nigger.* Although it was a routine and usually unemotional term for the people Faulkner grew up with, especially the white people, he recognized its intense offensiveness (at least when used without irony and in particular when used by whites—for it is still relatively unstigmatized as an ironical usage among blacks). When he takes up the story of Sutpen's "wild niggers," therefore, he speaks in the voice of the town, and, in a complicated tone, at once mocks the town's gullibility and admires its willingness to be hoodwinked, its pleasure in legends the townspeople only pretend to believe. With an ease that might well make us uneasy, Faulkner tries to have it both ways. He distances himself from the town's attitude, but he also enjoys giving voice to the attitudes he feels superior to.

In that spirit he introduces the story not as fact but rather as the "*legend* of Sutpen's wild negroes" (emphasis added), as the concoction of the half-ignorant, half-tomfool white citizens of Jefferson: "So the legend of the wild men came gradually back to town, brought by the men who would ride out to watch what was going on" (40). Repeatedly, Faulkner indicates that the townspeople misconstrue Sutpen's slaves: "The negroes could speak no English yet and doubtless there were more than Akers who did not know that the language in which they and Sutpen communicated was a sort of French and not some dark and fatal tongue of their own" (40–41). And again: "It took him two years, he and his crew of imported slaves which his adopted fellow citizens still looked on as being a good deal more deadly than any beast he could have started and slain in that country" (42–43). Sutpen, he says, "did not even need dogs to kill the game . . . but hunted it instead with human beings who belonged to him body and soul and of whom it was believed (or said) that they could creep up to a bedded buck and cut its throat before it could move" (45). Faulkner laughs at the townspeople's credulity even as he acknowledges—"(or said)"—that they laugh at it themselves.

Later, by contrast, Mr. Compson refers to the "wild niggers" (50) in a way that implies no critical distance on the expression or the legend, and soon he speaks in the same way of "house niggers" (55). Neither of those references appears in the manuscript, where the first is absent entirely and the other appears as "house servants," since in the manuscript Faulkner renders those scenes through the authorial voice rather than through Mr. Compson. Much later in the novel, as Quentin goes back over the story of Sutpen's early years, he returns rather luridly to the tale of "wild niggers" (273–74), but again in the voice of a character rather than in Faulkner's authorial voice, with Quentin at one point even attributing the words to his grandfather rather than taking credit for them himself (319–20).

Thus Mr. Compson, who takes over chapter 2, and the exterior narrator who begins it, have differing voices. They have things in common as well. Quentin's father sometimes refers to details already mentioned by the narrator, such as the men who no longer call Sutpen "Mister" (51, 49) or the number of stores in Jefferson (83, 35), suggesting that the narrator has been paraphrasing the first part of Mr. Compson's long monologue to Quentin and that Quentin hears from his father a more personal version of what we hear from the narrator. The paraphrase, then, softens the turn to Mr. Compson's tone of lazy erudition, of weary and sophisticated cynicism. "So at last civic virtue came to a boil" (51), he says, assuming an easy and ironical superiority to Jefferson citizens whom he hardly imagines as either civil or virtuous, certainly not in the old Roman sense of *civitas* or *virtus* that he would find in what the Appendix to *The Sound and the Fury* calls his "dog-eared Horaces and Livys."[3] Mr. Compson's first utterance—"Ah" (10)—repeated as his first word in chapter 3 (70), projects his air of leisurely and indulgent patience, wryly announcing his unsurprised pleasure at the chance to expatiate on a familiar legend. Upon that legend, in the coming chapters, he will unfurl his aesthete's jaded wisdom, his mock ardor for ironic truisms, his Latin and Greek from the veranda.

The emergence of Mr. Compson's voice and perspective proposes an alternative to Rosa's voice that so dominates chapter 1. When readers allow the voices to blur, they underestimate how Rosa and Mr. Compson each speak for a particular perspective and not for any authorial truth. Rosa's voice is taut, tense, angry, antithetical to Mr. Compson's worldly air of ease and leisure as he lounges after dinner on the front gallery, drawing at a cigar in the darkening evening (34). She is the outraged participant, he the amused spectator after the fact. His perspective implies that hers is distorted by her closeness to the Sutpens, even as hers implies a distortion in his distance.

Perhaps the most characteristic subject of Mr. Compson's cynicism is women. They have, he says, a natural "affinity for brigandage" (94). With patronizing irony, he picks a term of romanticized masculine transgression, even curling it sarcastically with a learned suffix ("brig-and*age*"). From his first words, even Mr. Compson himself seems unsure how seriously to take his wit against women: " 'Ah,' Mr. Compson said, 'Years ago we in the South made our women into ladies. Then the War came and made the ladies into ghosts. So what else can we do, being gentlemen, but listen to them being ghosts?' Then he said, 'Do you want to know the real reason why she chose you?' " (10). When suddenly he changes the subject, he seems to realize, a little defensively, that his words lack conviction. But they indicate the twists of confusion and leaps of assumption in so much that he will say through the novel. "Years ago," he begins, as if to displace responsibility onto the past and pretend that, sitting there on the gallery apart from things, he bears no responsibility for his wish to put "our" women in some category of special delicateness. For him, women's intellects and emotions don't much matter, but gallant gentlemen, as if out of pity, adopt a pose of mock helplessness ("what else can we do?") to humor these fragile ghosts in their inevitable unreasonableness. For Mr. Compson, the war came as if by itself; no one—least of all Southern men (or any men)—seems to have done anything to cause it. But the new burdens and in some ways liberating responsibilities that war imposes upon women, the stuff of postwar legend that turns up later in *Absalom, Absalom!,* he passes over in favor of the ghostly emptiness he can attribute to women by seeing war as a time when men take over. His final offer to give Quentin the "real reason" teases his son, since he goes on to say, as we have seen, that the real reason is that maybe the whole Sutpen story is Quentin's fault. His joke seems heartless, and yet also a father's loving needling, for it both takes advantage of Quentin's romantic susceptibilities and warns against them. The joke and the warning share in the same spiral of cynical irrelevance, taunting Quentin and making fun of Rosa's allegedly feminine detour, her relentless but incongruous logic.

When he digresses to lampoon someone else's runaway logic, he unwittingly submits himself to almost the same satire he turns on others. And his digressions underline the gratuitousness of his constant sneering at women, as when, with brilliant whirls of unprovoked, supposedly parenthetical enmity, he postpones completing a sentence for over half a page:

> Of the two men (I dont speak of Ellen, of course: in fact, you will notice that most divorces occur with women who were married by tobacco-chewing j.p.'s in country courthouses or by ministers waked after midnight, with their suspenders showing beneath their coattails and no collar on and a wife or spinster sister in curl papers for a witness. So is it too much to believe that these women come to long for divorce from a sense not of incompleteness but of actual frustration and betrayal? that regardless of the breathing evidence of children and all else, they still have in their minds even yet the

image of themselves walking to music and turning heads, in all the symbolical trappings and circumstances of ceremonial surrender of that which they no longer possess? and why not, since to them the actual and authentic surrender can only be (and have been) a ceremony like the breaking of a banknote to buy a ticket for the train)—of the two men, it was Sutpen. (57)

To Mr. Compson, women want divorce not because of anything men do or anything in their relation to men, but merely in lament for lost form, with their "frustration" comically not libidinal (in the usual sense of "frustration") so much as ritual. "These women," as he patronizingly groups them, want marriage not for "children and all else"—not for children, love, or sex—but for ceremony. They crave the "image" and the "symbolical" rather than what is imagined or symbolized. To Mr. Compson, women fancy themselves as objects of male desire, as the turners of heads rather than as actors in their own right who use ritual to express their own erotic or amorous desire. They attract male desire, but since, as he imagines, they have no desire of their own, they haven't the least interest in fulfilling or reciprocating what they attract. Mr. Compson's sense of feminine disinterest in the erotic expresses, as through a protective mask, his sense of male erotic ineffectuality—in psychoanalytic terms, castration anxiety. In Mr. Compson's castrated imagination, the erotic boundary that marriage ritualizes is, to women, a routine of bored and impersonally commercial exchange ("like the breaking of a banknote to buy a ticket") rather than a climax. None of this has anything to do with the Sutpens or Coldfields, but it tells a great deal about Mr. Compson as a lens that colors our view of the Sutpens and Coldfields.

It tells a great deal especially if we think also of Caroline and Caddy Compson, so familiar to readers of *The Sound and the Fury*. But they never appear in *Absalom, Absalom!* Faulkner gives readers of the earlier novel whole arenas of extra association that complicate the later novel but are not needed to follow it. Some readers choose rigidly to ignore all associations with *The Sound and the Fury,* while a few go to the opposite extreme and decline to talk about one book apart from the other. Perhaps we need not be so dogmatic in either direction. It seems reasonable enough for Faulkner to make *Absalom* capable of standing apart from *The Sound and the Fury* without wanting or even being able to shun absolutely the reverberations he can gain from alluding to it. And so readers of *The Sound and the Fury* and its belated Appendix can note that, as the dipsomaniac husband of his miserable hypochondriac wife, Mr. Compson has plenty of cause to feel sexually ineffectual, a feeling reinforced by his other failures— professional, financial, and perhaps paternal. He lets out some of his bitterness by verbally jabbing at his son over just what Quentin feels most sensitive to, namely, over Caddy and over women's supposedly casual attitude to their so-called loss of virginity, here figured tauntingly as the mere "breaking of a banknote to buy a ticket."

As usual, then, Mr. Compson's misogynist irony serves several purposes at once. It vents some vaguely motivated anger at women— vague in that we never learn much about Mr. Compson's past other than to see his spectacularly unlovable wife. It spars half-affectionately and half-cruelly at Quentin's edgy sensitivities, especially regarding his sister Caddy, which—at least in Quentin's own rationalizing—will lead Quentin to suicide nine months later, according to *The Sound and the Fury*. And it gives a view of the Sutpen and Coldfield past, a sometimes irritating view but nonetheless one that vividly contends for our sympathies. Indeed, the new momentum that Mr. Compson gives the narrative can lead us to forget that what he tells is his own view of things.

Mr. Compson's satirical scorn for women can highlight the way the events and emotions he describes are often not facts that he transmits so much as his own biased guesses about what might have happened: "Being a woman, she was doubtless one of that league of Jefferson women who . . . agreed never to forgive him. . . . Since the marriage was now a closed incident, she probably looked upon it as the one chance to thrust him back into the gullet of public opinion. . . . Or maybe women are even less complex than that and to them any wedding is better than no wedding" (61). "Doubtless," "probably," "maybe"—all Mr. Compson finds to work with here is his assumption that women all have the same attitude about men and marriage. But perhaps we should not take him so seriously, for he appears to adopt his humorous tone as a defense against being taken seriously, even by himself. Still, the defense only makes things worse, even though he himself hardly believes what he says. He believes only in its possibility and probability.

For Mr. Compson, and indeed for Faulkner, facts seem to distort truth. Or, since the very concepts of fact and truth are put in question, it will work better to say that to assert facts is to distort understanding. That denial of certain facts leads to a wildly overreaching style that can bewilder and horrify, especially if readers approach it humorlessly. Elsewhere Faulkner writes in tones and cadences much different from the orchestral sprawl of *Absalom, Absalom!*, and so the manner here has something to do with Mr. Compson, whose version of *Absalom*'s overreach, more relaxed than Rosa's, unleashes his own variation on the language that skeptics and bemused admirers sometimes dub *Faulknerese*. At one point, he starts to describe the child Rosa in a long sentence (77–79) that rolls on for half its 500 words before getting to much about young Rosa herself. He begins prosaically at her feet, but from there runs off to what her feet will be like, or rather, what they will *not* be like years later, and then to her furniture and soon to a flurry of things unconnected to Rosa's feet that her feet make him think of: "the small slight child whose feet, even when she would be grown, would never quite reach the floor even from her own chairs, the ones which she would inherit nor the ones—the objects—which she would accumulate as complement to and expression of individual character, as people do, as against Ellen who, though small-boned also, was what is known as fullbodied (and who would have been, if her life had not declined into a time when even men . . .)" and so on and on and on.

That sentence can suggest how Faulkner sees an object of description not by itself, not as a finished fact (note all the negatives—"never . . . nor . . . not"), but rather through its relation to a vast web of comparison with what it is not and never was or will be, and with what it was, will, would, might or could be, and not only for the character in question but also for other times, places, and characters. He sees every moment as if it lies at the hollow center of a vast three-dimensional asterisk of spoking possibilities and continuities that together express the incomprehensible moment more meaningfully than any direct statement. Indeed, he sees nothing by itself and instead sees everything relationally, so that his style at the level of sentence structure also fits the novel's temporal structure at large. In *Absalom, Absalom!*, Faulkner cannot look at the Sutpens simply in relation to the Sutpens or at the Compsons simply in relation to the Compsons. Instead, he obsessively sees the past through its relation to the present and the present through its relation to the past.

In chapter 3, therefore, Mr. Compson moves steadily farther from any pretense of factuality. "Perhaps," he begins one sentence, using one of his favorite words, Rosa "saw in her father's death . . .; perhaps she saw in this fate itself. . . . Perhaps she even saw herself as an instrument of retribution" (72). A great deal of Mr. Compson's tale telling comes introduced by words like *perhaps, probably, doubtless, I suppose.* Such speculations are specially though not exclusively Faulknerian. Faulkner gets the habit, in part, from Hawthorne. A word like *doubtless,* as in Hawthorne's "Young Goodman Brown," where Goody Cloyse makes her way through the forest "with singular speed for so aged a woman, and mumbling some indistinct words—a prayer, doubtless, as she went," can start to mean anything but doubtless. And words like *probably, perhaps,* and *suppose,* as much as they plea for Mr. Compson's modesty, also call attention to his overflow of lavish and improbable specificity.

He can pile a series of perhapses on one supposition, as above, to reiterate the point rhetorically. Or more radically, he can leap from one perhaps to another, spinning elaborate alternative suppositions even for trivial issues, as when he tries to explain why Sutpen didn't join his family and in-laws for the noon meal: "His reason may have been because of some delicacy for his father-in-law. . . . Or perhaps the reason was the one which Miss Rosa told you. . . . Or perhaps it was the reason which Sutpen gave himself . . ." (75–76). We might wonder if he even knows that Sutpen didn't join them for the noon meal in the first place and is supposing possible explanations for something that is itself only supposed. Readers are left to sort out the layering of possibility, to figure out the underlying Sutpen plot and the endless overlays of supposed plot, and also to figure out what those overlays tell about the twentieth-century characters who do the supposing. Readers are left to do all that, and yet not with so serious a face that we lose sight of the comedy in so indecipherable a palimpsest and of the pleasure that the characters take in adding yet another layer and another.

Apparently, Mr. Compson abides by the scattered outline of supposed facts, but in his extreme world of alternate maybes, so different from Rosa's furious bafflement, his own pleasure finally determines the past. In other words, his version of history, despite the vivid details (e.g., 82–83) that make it so hard to doubt, tells what he would *like* to have happened. "Only I have always liked to believe," he says to introduce one explanation, as later, when contemplating alternatives, he chooses the one that he calls "more likely, or so I would like to believe" (74, 94). And so another answer to the question, how does Mr. Compson know, is that he does *not* know. He makes it up.

SOME QUESTIONS ABOUT PLOT

All Mr. Compson's talk takes the basic story hardly beyond where Rosa Coldfield left it. Sutpen's past before he comes to Jefferson in 1833 remains vague, though we have a few hints. He comes from the south (35), brings a Spanish gold coin (38), and finds his architect in Martinique (39). His slaves speak French (41), and at age 14 he set out into the world with a fixed goal (62). For the most part, however, the outlines of plot still beg for explanation. Like a mystery or detective novelist, Faulkner gives effects before causes, and gives effects that cry out for causes. Here at the end of the first three chapters, it can help to take account of the mysteries of plot before going on to the chapters that follow. We will pause again for such an account at the close of the next two chapters of this study, looking back at our previous questions to see what has changed and how the changes matter.

At this point, Faulkner leaves four main questions about the Sutpen story after Sutpen comes to Jefferson in 1833: 1) why does Sutpen go to New Orleans? (85), 2) why does Henry vanish? (95–96), 3) why does Henry kill Charles Bon? and 4) why does Rosa not marry Sutpen?

The first question seems comparatively simple, since earlier in the same long sentence where Mr. Compson tells cryptically that Sutpen went to New Orleans he also mentions, for the first time, that Bon is from New Orleans. It is a point the book runs over quickly, but it can set off a host of other questions. Sutpen must suspect something about Bon, and more intently than a father ordinarily suspects his daughter's suitor. Given that Henry vanishes after talking to his father and later murders Bon, we might start to wonder. And so the first three of these questions seem closely related, and none of the narrators knows how to answer them. But the fourth question is different, because Rosa, presumably, knows why her engagement came apart, but she never mentions Sutpen's trip to New Orleans (which after all is a small detail) and is completely at a loss to understand why Henry disappeared and disavowed his birthright to run off with the very friend he later murders, again for no reason Rosa knows.

It can help, through the next chapters, to keep these questions in mind, and we will return to them as they evolve through the rest of the novel.

5

It's Just Incredible.
It Just Does Not Explain:
Chapters 4–5

Mr. Compson's Story

By chapter 4, we can recognize Mr. Compson's cynical voice, his pose as if from a surfeit of wisdom and experience: "So perhaps, now that God is an old man, He is not interested in the way we serve what you call lust" (143). And we can recognize his casual and luxuriant misogyny: "raised and trained to fulfill a woman's sole end and purpose: to love, to be beautiful, to divert. . . . No, not whores. Sometimes I believe that they are the only true chaste women, not to say virgins, in America" (145). The voice is familiar, but the plot, after circling and hovering for three chapters, at last leaps forward.

The forward movement can leave the impression that Mr. Compson answers the questions about plot that we saw as central by the end of chapter 3. Many first-time readers believe that he answers the first three of those questions, and some Faulkner critics proceed as if he does. According to Mr. Compson, Sutpen goes to New Orleans for the same reason suggested in chapter 3, to investigate Charles Bon, although he adds no particular reason why Sutpen would suspect Bon.

And according to Mr. Compson, in New Orleans Sutpen finds that Bon is already married—after the New Orleans fashion—to one of his own slaves, a pampered octoroon (one-eighth black, seven-eighths white) raised for concubinage. Then, on that Christmas Eve of 1860—still according to Mr. Compson—Sutpen tells Henry about Bon's marriage. Whereupon Henry, devoted to Bon, refuses to admit that he believes his father. Instead, he disavows home, family, and birthright and rides off with Bon to New Orleans where he learns about the octoroon at firsthand. Then, four years later, just as Bon returns to marry Judith, Henry kills him to prevent bigamy, kills him "dead as a beef," in the words Mr. Compson quotes from Wash Jones to close the chapter, words that bring home a violence that might before have seemed a little abstract, lost in the whirling blur of plot.

It's a great story. Even people who have read the novel before can succumb to Mr. Compson's hypnotically ornate tale and often react with shock when they realize, or remember, that Mr. Compson makes the story up. He tells a lavish tale of New Orleans, luxuriantly old and dark, baroquely sybaritic and abusive, but he doesn't even know that Henry Sutpen and Charles Bon rode off to New Orleans at all.

Much of what Mr. Compson imagines between Henry and Bon sounds intensely plausible, no less so because he makes it up. Still, he shapes his story not only by searching for what might plausibly fill in the scattered outline of hearsay, but also by assuming that part of the story must remain implausible. Because, as he tries to explain, the past is different from the present: "Yes, for them: of that day and time, of a dead time; people too as we are and victims too as we are, but victims of a different circumstance, simpler and therefore, integer for integer, larger, more heroic and the figures therefore more heroic too, not dwarfed and involved but distinct, uncomplex who had the gift of loving once or dying once instead of being diffused and scattered creatures drawn blindly limb from limb from a grab bag and assembled, author and victim too of a thousand homicides and a thousand copulations and divorcements" (109–10).

Mr. Compson takes a romantic view of the past and a modernist view of the present. For him, the people of the past seem more distinct, that is, more understandable. It is not clear what makes him think so. In part, he rationalizes and even apologizes for the story he is getting set to tell about Henry and Bon and New Orleans, for by itself that story seems implausibly simple. As Mr. Compson goes on to acknowledge, Bon's morganatic marriage to an octoroon slave might disturb the kind of backwoods prig that he guesses Henry must be, but prig or not, it would hardly seem momentous to a plantation heir of Henry's world, where white men's sexual appropriation of black women was taken for granted. Certainly it would not loom large next to the murder it is supposed to explain, the murder of a white aristocrat and idolized mentor. But it is hard to tell whether Mr. Compson's idea that the people of the past are blunter and simpler comes from a sense of *inherent* difference or from a sense that the past only *feels* different because we peer at it across a canyon of lost time. Either way, it is a convenient idea for him, because his assumption that we can understand the past buttresses the story he is about to offer and veils that he himself makes up that story. And so he tells Quentin that "perhaps any more light than" the "single globe stained and bug-fouled . . . which even when clean gave off but little light 'would be too much' " (109, 110) to shine on Judith's letter from Bon, as if closer scrutiny might break down his romantic vision of a simpler, larger, more heroic past.

It seems, finally, that his vision of the past as purer and grander has less to do with any scrutiny of the past—there is, after all, little left to scrutinize, and he is reluctant to look at even this isolated document under bright light—than with his wish to set the past against the present. He wants to protect the past from the present's complexities and protect the present from the romantic simplicities that he projects onto the past. Therefore, his vision of the past tells about his vision of the present. For him, the present is dwarfed, involved, complex, condemned to an abysmally demoralizing repetition, its people loving and dying again and again in a scattered and blind diffusion that saps away its meaning and leaves only an endless and ordinary series. The

romance he imagines in murder and love gives way to a dryer litany—
in a language almost from the census bureau—of homicides, copulations, and divorcements. Instead of the wholeness, "integer for integer," that he attributes to a romantic past, Mr. Compson's present is
a modernist assemblage of the arbitrary, the haphazard, the purposeless
("blindly . . . from a grab bag"), of interruptions ("homicides and
divorcements"), and of completions that never complete ("a thousand
copulations" indistinguishable from homicides and divorcements). In
a word, Mr. Compson's vision of the present is a vision of failure.

He should know, if we judge by *The Sound and the Fury,* including
its Appendix, which can make Mr. Compson's words here sound yet
more aimed at the present and barbed for Quentin. The last thing that
Quentin, thinking about Caddy, wants to hear is that copulation or
the repetition of copulation becomes boringly meaningless and banal,
or that nowadays no one can love just once—whether that means that
Caddy will drift through an endless series of tiresome copulations or
that he himself could some day love someone besides Caddy. More
subtly, as he looks toward his suicide and romantically imagines it as
a dreamy apotheosis of earthly desire, Quentin hardly wants to hear
that dying, even homicide, is no more romantic than his father's cynical
idea of love or (in his father's ironic Latinism) copulation.

Mr. Compson, ostensibly concerned with the Sutpens, never lets
up his indirect and seemingly incidental taunting of his son. He says
that Henry's "fierce provincial's pride in his sister's virginity was a
false quantity which must incorporate in itself an inability to endure
in order to be precious, to exist, and so must depend upon its loss,
absence, to have existed at all. In fact," he goes on, "perhaps this is
the pure and perfect incest" (118–19). Such comments would rub
rawly against Quentin's anguish for Caddy. Perhaps Mr. Compson
feels that his teasing can set Quentin right, can make him stop mistaking
the ordinary (Caddy's sexuality) for the momentous. But *Absalom,
Absalom!* includes so little direct address to these preoccupations of
The Sound and the Fury that Faulkner leaves us unable to describe Mr.
Compson's motives, though we can certainly see his determination to

provoke. Through one veiled reference after another, whether to the young women around Oxford—Judith's cohorts—as so many "interchangeable provincial virgins" (134), to Bon's paying "Judith the dubious compliment of not even trying to ruin her" (121), or to the "other sex" as "separated into three sharp divisions . . .—the virgins whom gentlemen someday married, the courtesans . . . , the slave girls and women upon whom that first caste rested and to whom in certain cases it doubtless owed the very fact of its virginity" (135), Mr. Compson's misogynist wit takes on a quality of morbid humor. Talking to his son, he goes so far as to wonder if "it was not the fact of the mistress and child, the possible bigamy, to which Henry gave the lie, but to the fact that it was his father who told him, his father who anticipated him, the father who is the natural enemy of any son" (129).

These oblique but wry allusions to Judith as analogous to Caddy imply also an analogy between Quentin and Henry. Together with the sense that Henry's killing of Judith's suitor recalls Quentin's wish to kill Dalton Ames in *The Sound and the Fury,* they encourage Quentin to identify with Henry, hence drawing Quentin, despite his silence, further into the story and slowly stoking him for some kind of reaction.

Judith, however, unlike anything we have yet seen from her father, mother, brother, or still shadowy half-sister, enters Mr. Compson's story to speak for herself apart from what he imagines she *might* say. Though Mr. Compson and his mother mediate her words, she challenges his notion that the past is simpler and more certain:

> Because you make so little impression, you see. You get born and you try this and you dont know why only you keep on trying it and you are born at the same time with a lot of other people, all mixed up with them, like trying to, having to, move your arms and legs with strings only the same strings are hitched to all the other arms and legs and the others all trying and they don't know why either except that the strings are all in one another's way like five or six people all trying to make a rug on the same loom only each one wants to weave his own pattern into the rug; and it cant matter, you know that, or the Ones that set up the loom would have arranged

things a little better, and yet it must matter because you keep on trying or having to keep on trying and then all of a sudden it's all over. (157)

This contradicts Mr. Compson's notion that people in the past were simple, heroic integers. As Judith sees them, they are "all mixed up" in a tangle like Mr. Compson's image of people in the present as "diffused and scattered creatures drawn blindly limb from limb." Of course, Judith sees the past differently because Mr. Compson's past is her present, but she conceives even the concept of pastness in plainer, less romantic terms. "You try," says Judith, but "it cant matter." Still, you try anyway, and then it's simply over. In its abrupt demise, the past, to Judith, is simply gone, without its disappearance leaving any cloak of romance or heroism.

Even so, in a passage that takes on extra poignance if we see it as also pointing to Faulkner's own urge to write, she sees the writing in Bon's letter as one way to preserve at least something from the past:

And so maybe if you could go to someone, the stranger the better, and give them something—a scrap of paper—something, anything, it not to mean anything in itself and them not even to read it or keep it, not even bother to throw it away or destroy it, at least it would be something just because it would have happened, be remembered even if only from passing from one hand to another, one mind to another, and it would be at least a scratch, something, something that might make a mark on something that *was* once for the reason that it can die someday, while the block of stone cant be *is* because it never can become *was* because it cant ever die or perish. (158)

To Judith, not so cynically distant as Mr. Compson, though no more epistemologically confident, the present is defined not *against* the past, as for him, but *by* the past, by its capacity to become past, by perishability, fluidity, and by its potential, at least, for reading and interpretation. To Judith, it is enough for the past to be subject only to an unrecoverable lost reading, as the whole story of the Sutpens might be unrecoverable for Mr. Compson and Quentin and the readers of *Absalom, Absalom!*

We are left to ask, then, in what light to take Mr. Compson's explanation of why Henry repudiated his home in favor of his friend—and then murdered the friend. Many readers get so caught up in Mr. Compson's story that they overlook how he mixes his explanation with reasons to doubt it. For one thing, it isn't like Sutpen to take off on a 600-mile journey to investigate a man his daughter has just met, "this in a man who might have challenged and shot someone whom he disliked or feared but would not have made even a ten mile journey to investigate him" (125). Mr. Compson assumes that Henry would believe what his father says on that Christmas Eve, apparently because it would be too farfetched to lie about, and that Henry denies his belief and rides off with Bon out of a young man's more or less ordinary preference for friend over father and for passion over uneasy truth. But then, why would he ride off to New Orleans, where he was bound to discover the truth he had committed himself to deny? "What else could he have hoped to find in New Orleans, if not the truth, if not what his father had told him, what he had denied and refused to accept even though, despite himself, he must have already believed? But who knows why a man, though suffering, clings, above all the other well members, to the arm or leg which he knows must come off? Because he loved Bon" (111). To give in to the father's power would be castratingly to deny his own power, but to attempt to deny the father's power and then go ahead and confirm it anyway is the immature kind of false compromise that emotion strikes with evidence. And the emotion, Mr. Compson therefore assumes, is that Henry loves Bon.

Mr. Compson sketches a convincing scene of how one emotion leads to another, but it's a rough sketch, given how little evidence he has. His picture of men agonizing over their manhood has a sound of Compson worry that might feel at odds with Sutpen assurance, unless the Sutpens look assured only from a distance, or unless Henry, as a next-generation Sutpen, is more like a Compson. Mr. Compson doesn't know, and it's easy enough and maybe even plausible enough for him to write off as love what he doesn't understand.

It's Just Incredible. It Just Does Not Explain

Mr. Compson himself admits that his story would make no sense to Bon, who would see as perfectly unremarkable what Henry apparently finds horrible enough to call for murder, a "situation in which probably all his [Bon's] contemporaries who could afford it were likewise involved and which it would no more have occurred to him to mention to his bride or wife or to her family than he would have told them the secrets of a fraternal organization which he had joined before he married" (114). Indeed, the Charles Bon of Mr. Compson's tale is as improbable as the Henry Sutpen, for it is hard to believe that, as a 30-or-so-year-old metropolitan from a wealthy French New Orleans family he would leave his elegant world of ease for a tiny backwoods college newly sprouted in the wilderness. Mr. Compson supposes that Bon accepts his incomprehensible place "for a reason obviously good enough to cause him to endure it and apparently too serious or at least too private to be divulged to what acquaintances he now possessed" (121) and studies law "since only that could have made his residence bearable, regardless of what reason he may have brought with him for remaining" (126). Why law would be any more bearable Mr. Compson never explains (the Appendix to *The Sound and the Fury* later gives law as Mr. Compson's own profession, though he hardly troubles to follow it), but that only underlines the mystery about why Bon would go to the University of Mississippi in the first place, which the long tale of the trip to New Orleans and the casual marriage to the octoroon does nothing to explain. It can make us wonder whether any explanation of why Henry repudiates his family and murders his friend might not need to account for more than Mr. Compson tries to. And so it helps to insist that the people of the past were simpler, if all you can think of to explain them are stories not complicated enough to account for what you have to explain.

But even Mr. Compson knows that simplicity cannot excuse a story that won't fit together. "Yes," he says, "granted that, even to the unworldly Henry, let alone the more travelled father, the existence of the eighth part negro mistress and the sixteenth part negro son, granted even the morganatic ceremony—a situation which was as much a part of a wealthy young New Orleanian's social and fashionable equipment as his dancing slippers—was reason enough, which is drawing honor a little fine even for the shadowy paragons which are our ancestors born in the South and come to man- and womanhood about eighteen sixty or sixty one. It's just incredible. It just does not explain" (123–24). If Rosa's words "without rhyme or reason or shadow of excuse" provide a touchstone for her inability to explain the story, so these words of Mr. Compson's suggest a touchstone for his failure to explain it in a believable way. Unlike Rosa, he offers an explanation, and an elaborately detailed one, but "it's just incredible. It just does not explain."

As if stung by his failure, he wanders into a long speculation that expands to address the impassioned inquiry of *Absalom, Absalom!* as a whole, implying that maybe not just the story of the Sutpens but even the larger past they are only a part of can never give way to our drive to understand it: "Or perhaps that's it: they dont explain and we are not supposed to know. We have a few old mouth-to-mouth tales; we exhume from old trunks and boxes and drawers letters without salutation or signature, in which men and women who once lived and breathed are now merely initials or nicknames . . . ; we see dimly people . . . in this shadowy attenuation of time possessing now heroic proportions, performing their acts of simple passion and simple violence, impervious to time and inexplicable" (124). Here Mr. Compson returns to his idea that the past is simpler, except that now the simplicity seems more clearly an illusion of distance, a confession of mysteries that seem less complex only because time has made them inaccessible. "Yes," he goes on:

> Judith, Bon, Henry, Sutpen: all of them. They are there, yet something is missing; they are like a chemical formula exhumed along with the letters from that forgotten chest, carefully, the paper old and failing and falling to pieces, the writing faded, almost indecipherable, yet meaningful, familiar in shape and sense, the name and presence of volatile and sentient forces; you bring them together in the proportions called for, but nothing happens; you re-read, tedious and intent, poring, making sure that you have forgotten nothing,

made no miscalculation; you bring them together again and again
nothing happens: just the words, the symbols, the shapes themselves,
shadowy inscrutable and serene, against that turgid background of
a horrible and bloody mischancing of human affairs. (124)

To Mr. Compson, we struggle between a sense that the past is
inherently inaccessible and a sense that, with enough effort, we can
recalculate, pick out some missing piece and fit everything together.[1]
He feels tempted to think people can understand the past if they
simply try hard enough. But the effort never quite blossoms into the
understanding it seems to promise. Instead, he finds only words, and
words that, as before, he reads more skeptically than Judith does. To
him, the words feel empty when gauged against the bloody chaos
around them too horrible and arbitrary to permit any satisfaction in
meaning. As in Rosa's befuddled tale, we have the effect without the
cause, a "curious lack of economy between cause and effect" (147), a
surplus of symbol but a scarcity of knowledge to be symbolized. Mr.
Compson doesn't know, and occasionally he admits as much: "and
none to ever know just why or just what happened between Henry and
his father" (130).

Since he doesn't know, the things he makes up reflect his own self.
And what he imagines most is Bon: "He is the curious one to me"
(114). As the character they know least about, Bon gives Mr. Compson
the freest range, until his imagined Bon sounds like an aestheticized
and idealized version of Mr. Compson himself, languishing in eloquent
and cynical lassitude here in *Absalom* or even more in *The Sound and
the Fury* and its Appendix. "Or perhaps," he says, reclining on the
veranda and casting his jaded wisdom at his young son, "(I like to
think this) . . . the man [Bon] reclining in a flowered, almost feminised
gown . . . this man handsome elegant and even catlike and too old to
be where he was, too old not in years but in experience, with some
tangible effluvium of knowledge, surfeit: of actions done and satiations
plumbed and pleasures exhausted and even forgotten" (117), "this
indolent man too old to find even companionship among the youths,

the children, with whom he now lived; this man miscast for the time and knowing it, accepting it" (121). Even when Mr. Compson's Bon speaks, he sounds like Quentin's father. Trying to convince Henry, whom Mr. Compson imagines as the backwoods bumpkin with scruples, Mr. Compson's Bon defends his pleasure with the octoroon slave as a "perfectly normal human instinct which you Anglo-Saxons insist upon calling lust and in whose service you revert in sabbaticals to the primordial caverns" (143), an attitude and even a set of words that come from the same cynical intelligence as Mr. Compson's references to Jefferson religion as "that aptitude and eagerness of the Anglo-Saxon for complete mystical acceptance of immolated sticks and stones" (67), or to Henry's awestruck abashment as "that heritage peculiarly Anglo-Saxon—of fierce proud mysticism and that ability to be ashamed of ignorance and inexperience" (134).

And so when Mr. Compson repeatedly insists—from the first words of his story in chapter 4—that "Henry loved Bon" (110), he not only sets going a theory of Henry's motives, but also invokes his own envy for the fantasies that he imagines Bon fulfills. When he envisions Henry looking rapturously "upon Bon as though he were a hero out of some adolescent Arabian Nights who had stumbled upon . . . the ability and opportunity to pass from the scene of one scarce imaginable delight to the next one without interval or pause or satiety" (118), we can hear the echo of his own desire more than any plausible picture of life at a new college in the wilderness. In one sense, Mr. Compson's envy of the Bon he imagines recalls the Sutpen he earlier imagined, for his Sutpen, and Rosa's, looms like his Bon as a figure of envy, a titan from some grand founder myth who springs suddenly from nowhere with nothing and then mysteriously transmutes that nothing into fabulous extravagance. It is a classic fantasy: a release from the confinement of parents and a past. Thus, suave as Bon seems next to Sutpen's clumsy arrogance, when Mr. Compson imagines that Bon "must have appeared almost phoenix-like, full-sprung from no childhood, born of no woman and impervious to time" (90), he makes Bon sound much like Sutpen, or at least like Sutpen as he appears to the people of Jefferson.

That is, however, a fantasy that Mr. Compson cannot sustain, since he sends Bon—with Henry—back where he came from, New Orleans. Like his vision of Bon, his vision of Bon's city comes shaped by unreflected-upon routines of association. He says "I can imagine" nine times in this chapter and six times in this one episode, but his imagination follows familiar cultural patterns. He assimilates New Orleans to stereotypes of the luxuriously foreign, exotic, even Oriental ("Arabian Nights"), and to related stereotypes of decadent wealth and the feminine—as if the feminine were somehow the dissipated embodiment of some opulent and inherent "other." For him New Orleans is the antithesis of Yoknapatawpha, more his own wish-dream than a place that two young men might travel to in 1861: "that city foreign and paradoxical, with its atmosphere at once fatal and languorous, at once feminine and steelhard" (134), the "architecture a little curious, a little femininely flamboyant and therefore to Henry opulent, sensuous, sinful" (136). It is a city of lush secrets and erotic promise, harboring the feminine and the femininely interior: "and now, the solid gates closed behind them instead of before, no sight or evidence above the high thick walls of the low city and scarce any sound of it, the labyrinthine mass of oleander and jasmine, lantana and mimosa walling yet again the strip of bare earth combed and curried" (139–40). Deep in the labyrinth waits the cherished and abused embodiment of exotic paradox: a "woman with a face like a tragic magnolia, the eternal female, the eternal Who-suffers" (141), the denizen of the irrational, the ultimately feminine with her very femininity defined by her victimization.

The fantasy crescendos in slavery, for the feminine in itself is only part of the fantasized other: "something of secret and curious and unimaginable delights. Without his knowing what he saw it was as though to Henry the blank and scaling barrier in dissolving produced and revealed not comprehension to the mind . . . , but striking instead straight and true to some primary blind and mindless foundation of all young male living dream and hope—a row of faces like a bazaar of flowers, the supreme apotheosis of chattelry, of human flesh bred of the two races for that sale—a corridor of doomed and tragic flower faces" (138).

The woman most "other," in Mr. Compson's dream—a dream that is anything but his own, a dream from a larger, white cultural yearning that he voices—is not only woman but also dark. And she is not simply black—except by the legal dualism that makes anyone of any African ancestry an exploitable other—not simply black but rather tinged white. The darker trace can expose how the repressed ("blind and mindless") role of the other is to objectify something denied in the white self—denied, and yet so desperately sought that it must be exteriorized as some "other" before it can be looked at and yearned for. Mr. Compson's haughty insistence that Henry doesn't know what he sees masks his own submission to a larger cultural desire beyond his brilliant but provincial comprehension, for we are all embedded in the unconscious cultural fantasies that structure our secret wishes and our most mundane assumptions and routines.

Something at once so feared and so ached for might seem controlled—and yet still alluringly exterior and other—if it can be bought, made into a commodity. Hence the "bazaar of flowers," which speaks of manipulative and objectifying commerce, and yet also of the mythically, orientally exotic, the supposedly dark and inscrutable. Bon—as Mr. Compson imagines him—recognizes (if he does not understand) his fascination with the mix of white and black, but feebly insists on denying the economics:

> white blood to give the shape and pigment of what the white man calls female beauty, to a female principle which existed, queenly and complete, in the hot equatorial groin of the world long before that white one of ours came down from trees and washed its hair and bleached out—a principle apt docile and instinct with strange and ancient curious pleasures of the flesh (which is all: there is nothing else) which her white sisters of a mushroom yesterday flee from in moral and outraged horror—a principle which, where her white sister must needs try to make an economic matter of it like someone who insists upon installing a counter or a scales or a safe in a store or business for a certain percentage of the profits, reigns, wise supine and all-powerful, from the sunless and silken bed which is her throne. No. Not whores: Not even courtesans. (144)

This associates feminine essence with the black and the crudely Darwinian. (*The Origin of Species* came out in 1859 and *The Descent of Man* in 1871, well before Mr. Compson imagines Bon's words, but 10 years after Bon would have spoken them.) And it associates black essence with some purer, primal sexuality, much as Faulkner does still more luridly in *Light in August* when he refers to the "fecundmellow voices of negro women" as murmuring of a return to the "lightless hot wet primogenitive Female."[2] To set off black sexuality, Mr. Compson's Bon pits what he sees as the castrating boredom, the sexual disinterest of active white women against the "docile" impassivity that seems to him a precondition for the erotic. Such need for preconditions exposes the vision as Mr. Compson's own dream of power and escape from his own impassivity (even more visible in *The Sound and the Fury,* where we see him impotent before his scolding, hypochondriac wife), which he projects onto the submission of the black and feminine.

The enslaved concubines' submission, of course, is coerced rather than, as Mr. Compson's Bon suggests, characteristic and instinctual. He figures the black concubines' impassivity by their alleged indifference to the economic, when on the contrary they are forcibly secluded from economic choice, and secluded not by the entrepreneurial cravings of white women but rather by men like Bon who, despite his protestations, submit their sexual slaves to the "counter" and "scales" of a market ("bazaar") that fixes an exact monetary reckoning on each face in the row of human flowers. To complete the travesty, he labels these slaves "all-powerful," although theirs is only the pedestaled false power of the "sunless and silken," the coddled and cloistered. Mr. Compson, who attributes such ironies to the character he imagines, partly sees through the denials. In a sense, he takes Bon himself as seeing partly through them, since he imagines Bon saying such things less to concoct a defense of slavery and concubinage than to put something over on Henry.

Such mixed possibilities make a complicated layering, one that will grow still more complicated later in the novel. When Bon defends the breeding and marketing of women like his octoroon because "they are more valuable as commodities than white girls, raised and trained to fulfill a woman's sole end and purpose: to love, to be beautiful, to divert" (145), it is not Bon who speaks. It is Mr. Compson. Still, it is not necessarily Mr. Compson speaking his own ideas, not even indirectly or unconsciously, though of course it could be. Instead, these words show what, from the limits and biases of his own desires and capacities, Mr. Compson imagines Bon might have said in circumstances that Mr. Compson only imagines might have happened. Even as the imagined words of an imagined Bon, they do not necessarily indicate the hypothetical Bon's beliefs so much as what Bon might think it would help him to say. Yet they are galling words to direct at Henry, since Henry's concern here is for Judith, and Bon's relation to Judith. The same words, then, that from one side of Bon's imagined perspective seem aimed to calm Henry, to coax him not to worry about Bon's connection to the other woman, from another side of Bon's imagined perspective taunt Henry's urge to protect his sister. They paint her and all women as good only to be a man's salacious plaything, and they paint her fiancé as interested in her only as such a plaything. At the same time, though, since all this comes from Mr. Compson to Quentin rather than from Bon to Henry, it is also Mr. Compson's taunt at Quentin's sensitivities over Caddy, for which Henry's sensitivities at times seem little more than a stand-in.

And so Mr. Compson's tale of the Sutpens cannot be trusted. If chapter 4 at first seems to extend the plot, then the more we ponder the extensions the airier they seem. By the end, even Quentin stops listening (159, 160). But all that for nothing? Or for no more than the interesting, to be sure, but not exactly to-the-point insights about garrulous Mr. Compson himself, which we already had a good start on from earlier chapters? Quentin, however, stops listening not because of any emptiness in his father's tale, but because it forcefully sets his own thoughts astir. No scrutiny of the private motives behind his father's story can reduce its interest as sheer story, which is, after all, what any novel is anyway. Such scrutiny only shifts the light in which we see the tale.

It's Just Incredible. It Just Does Not Explain

Mr. Compson still conjures up a wonderful portrait of Creole Louisiana. It recalls *Uncle Tom's Cabin*, where we hear the lavish story of a slave from exactly the same concubine's world as Bon's octoroon. A similar ambiance turns up in the fiction of other New Orleans writers like George Washington Cable, Lafcadio Hearn, or Kate Chopin. Faulkner may have read those novelists or others like them (though probably not Chopin, who was largely forgotten); he would certainly have heard tales like theirs when he lived in New Orleans, especially from his friend Lyle Saxon, who wrote romantic histories of Louisiana, New Orleans, and the New Orleans French Quarter.[3] Such scenes as the long tragicomic depiction of Bon introducing Henry to the sybaritic New Orleans world and his octoroon morganatic wife, or the drums, fiddles, flags, and tears account of the gathering University soldiers (151–53) do not go away once we realize that Mr. Compson makes them up, especially since, whether Mr. Compson makes them up or not, Mr. Faulkner certainly does. Mr. Compson's story is so lush with evocative detail that, within the limits of a fiction, it becomes hard not to believe. It retains its own unrejectable truth as story, for it has the only authority that cannot be undermined: the authority of fiction.

Then at last, as the chapter moves to its end, Quentin reads the letter his father has held before them through the whole story, and Charles Bon, it turns out, writes exactly as Mr. Compson talks, and with exactly the ornate aesthete's lugubrious irony and the fatalist's determination that Mr. Compson has attributed to him, attributed— we can now see—perhaps with that very letter as cue. And thus, despite Mr. Compson's extravagant bias and indulgent turning of the story to his own conscious and unconscious purposes, we should not, after all, hurry to dismiss what he tells us.

NARRATIVE STRUCTURE AND ROSA'S UNSPEAKABLE MONOLOGUE

Bon's letter, introduced and followed by Mr. Compson's words and an exterior or authorial voice, shifts the perspective slightly, but the narrative structure of chapter 4 presents no particular difficulties. The last words of the chapter snap tightly onto the last words of the previous chapter. The manuscript indicates that Faulkner wrote the longer version, which now concludes chapter 4, for the end of chapter 3, and later decided to postpone the last sentences and leave the end of chapter 3 hanging with Wash's shout " 'Air you Rosie Coldfield?' "[4] That way he could sustain even that small suspense and close chapter 4 by returning to Wash's irreverent, slangy interruption, this time staying for the lurid news: "Air you Rosie Coldfield? Then you better come on out yon. Henry has done shot that durn French feller. Kilt him dead as a beef" (107, 165)—dramatic final words for a chapter that has focused more or less rapturously on that durn French feller and Henry's love for him, all in the effort to fathom why Henry would shoot the friend he loves.

In chapter 5, however, the language and narrative structure turn immeasurably more complicated. For one thing, chapter 5 falls, chronologically, between chapters 1 and 2 (see the appendix). Even when readers miss that somersault, the delay makes them reach chapter 5 with a more developed interest in the characters and events than if Faulkner had kept to chronological sequence and gone directly from chapter 1 to chapter 5. That makes readers more willing to put up with and even enjoy the chapter's extraordinary difficulties. And chapter 5 suddenly gives close attention to the two Sutpen women who have so far hovered almost silently in the background, Judith and Clytie, whom readers are liable to approach with the heightened interest wrought by delay and suspense.

When I ask my students what is the narrative voice of chapter 5, they say Rosa Coldfield. After I ask if they're sure, and they say they are, then I ask if we can really imagine Rosa *speaking* such stuff as we find in a couple sample passages. When I take a deep breath and read the passages out loud, students often break into a laughter that suggests their relief at the encouragement to take the ponderous bombast of chapter 5 a little skeptically. To be sure, in such a case I have primed them for a particular response, but it seems to me that the laughter, even if released by a teacher's nudge, holds more insight than the dutifully academic assertion about which character does the narrating. For it is difficult to imagine a character, even a Faulkner character, even Rosa Coldfield, literally *speaking* the words of *Absalom's* chapter 5, at least not in any ordinary sense, not even any ordinarily fictional sense:

> *But root and urge I do insist and claim, for had I not heired too from all the unsistered Eves since the Snake? Yes, urge I do: warped chrysalis of what blind perfect seed: for who shall say what gnarled forgotten root might not bloom yet with some globed concentrate more globed and concentrate and heady-perfect because the ne-glected root was planted warped and lay not dead but merely slept forgot?* (179)

> *Because I who had learned nothing of love, not even parents' love— that fond dear constant violation of privacy, that stultification of the burgeoning and incorrigible I which is the meed and due of all mammalian meat, became not mistress, not beloved, but more than even love; I became all polymath love's androgynous advocate.* (182)

Now this is stirring stuff, but not even Rosa, in any other chapter, talks with such farfetched intensity and eloquence. I call this chapter Rosa's "unspeakable monologue," so as to indicate the abstract, impossible sense in which she speaks what cannot be spoken. Its strangeness seems to develop out of similar experiments in earlier Faulkner novels. Faulkner narrates a whole section of *The Sound and the Fury* from the perspective of an "idiot," an adult so retarded that he cannot use language for speech or even thought. Yet Faulkner gives him a language that aspires to represent not only what he inarticulately feels (which would be fairly routine, since we all have feelings we cannot voice), but also the abstract condition of what the idiot would say if he could say anything even though—and this must come across too— he can't. From there *The Sound and the Fury* moves to another section that recounts Quentin Compson's thoughts—in first-person—on the day of his suicide, even though, in a stunningly self-evident paradox, Quentin doesn't live to recount them. Again in *As I Lay Dying,* Faulkner tells one section in the words of a dead character, and most of *As I Lay Dying* seems to be narrated in some sort of pure voice that comes out of particular characters but not out of any particular time or place.

In *Absalom, Absalom!* Rosa is, to say the least, anything but dead and anything but an idiot, but in this chapter she still "speaks" in a language beyond her capacity for speech as we think of it in ordinarily realistic fiction. Yet she speaks in the ordinary sense as well, for we're told that Quentin is not listening (215, 216), and by a comically reverse logic, if there are words he is not listening to, then she must be talking. Her "speech" thus represents not only what she says to Quentin, but also something more deeply interior and linguistically resourceful. It may make us think of Mr. Compson's remark that "perhaps that is what went on, not in Henry's mind but in his soul" (119) or his idea that Henry and Bon exchange thoughts in a "dialogue without words, speech" (137). More pertinently, Rosa herself, right in chapter 5, recalls that she and Clytie glared at each other *"as though we spoke to one another free of the limitations and restrictions of speech and hearing"* (172), which describes the emotional tenacity and the simplicity-be-damned syntax of this chapter and fits Faulkner's decision to signal a special voice by putting Rosa's "speech" in italics without quotation marks. The italics distinguish the absence of quotation marks from their absence in Mr. Compson's more meandering and less driven eloquence in chapter 3. There Mr. Compson speaks the words in the ordinary sense of spoken language, whereas here, although the words bear some relation to what Rosa supposedly tells Quentin, they also represent a version more stringent and uncompromising than speech can render.

ALL POLYMATH LOVE'S ANDROGYNOUS ADVOCATE

What kind of character is this now more intense Rosa Coldfield, self-dubbed "all polymath love's androgynous advocate"? Many readers get so swept into her knotted-up fervor that they pass by questions they might ask about any other narrative, especially one angled through a particular character's perspective. Rosa has not drawn as much critical scrutiny as the other major characters; nor has chapter 5 drawn as much as the other chapters. Perhaps it can help to begin by comparing Rosa's facts to Mr. Compson's facts.

To Mr. Compson, Charles Bon seems "shadowy: a myth, a phantom. . . . Yet there was the body which Miss Rosa saw" (128). He doesn't know that earlier that afternoon, though later in the novel's narrative, Rosa says (albeit while speaking "beyond the limitations of speech and hearing"), *"I never saw him. I never even saw him dead"* (181, 187), and makes a special point of describing how it feels to have missed him (187–90). Mr. Compson's long story filling out the phantom Bon makes her hesitation in astonished ignorance seem almost modest. On that point, Rosa has the advantage in knowledge though not in imagination, though it is only the knowledge of her own ignorance.

But on another bit of knowledge, Mr. Compson has the advantage. They both say that Henry murdered Bon. Rosa cannot imagine why, whereas Mr. Compson imagines or decides that Henry did it to prevent Bon from committing bigamy by marrying Judith, though Mr. Compson himself finds that "just incredible. It just does not explain." Incredible or not, he thrice describes how Judith discovers the bigamy (or, if she already knows, then how she is reminded) when she finds a telltale picture on her fiancé's corpse. He describes Bon as "this man who was at least an intending bigamist even if not an out and out blackguard, and on whose dead body four years later Judith was to find the photograph of the other woman and the child" (110, 112, 116–17).

Rosa seems like someone who would feel appalled at the mere issue of bigamy, let alone the act, but she never breathes a hint of it. Rosa tells a different story:

> *And this too they cannot tell you: How I ran, fled, up the stairs and found no grieving widowed bride but Judith standing . . . holding*

something in one hanging hand; and if there had been grief or anguish she had put them too away, complete or not complete I do not know, along with that unfinished wedding dress. 'Yes, Rosa?' she said, . . . and I stopped in running's midstride again though my body, blind unsentient barrow of deluded clay and breath, still advanced: And how I saw that what she held in that lax and negligent hand was the photograph, the picture of herself in its metal case which she had given him, held casual and forgotten against her flank. (176–77)

In a turn half-sad and half-comic, like so much that we learn about Rosa in chapter 5, she doesn't know about the bigamy. Charging up the stairs to find what she has already imagined, she simply assumes that the photograph is of Judith. Rosa is more "deluded," as she puts it, than she realizes, for she cannot see the irony of grief and anguish in Judith's anything but "lax and negligent" clinging to that telltale photograph.

Or should we doubt Mr. Compson's version? Maybe, but he never puts it in the elaborate frame of mere possibility that he admits to for the journey to New Orleans or the words between Henry and Thomas Sutpen on Christmas Eve. By contrast, his knowing about the picture at all indicates that somehow he has found something out. Perhaps he knows about it only because Quentin reports what Rosa said that afternoon, and then, after his fashion, Mr. Compson embellishes that sliver of detail. But he must have some knowledge of the New Orleans woman, since the point of his story is to build her into a motive grand enough to lead Henry to murder Bon. Indeed, it will turn out in chapter 6 that Grandfather Compson later saw the New Orleans woman and her son, deciphered who they were, and told Quentin's father, though we never hear anything more about the photograph.[5] Even if we cannot say that the New Orleans octoroon's picture is either Mr. Compson's embellishment or something he somehow knows, the point is that he knows about Bon's morganatic marriage and makes it the pivot of the story, whereas Rosa knows nothing about it and feels bewildered at the lack of explanation, the lack of "rhyme or reason or shadow of excuse." By the time we read about Rosa's befuddlement in chapter 5, things have changed from when we read about it in chapter 1, because we now have the modest advantage over Rosa of Mr. Compson's elaborate explanation. It may be "just incredible," but it sets off questions that change our reading.

It thus helps to place where Rosa stands in relation to the story's meager net of fact, but the difficulty of her personality and prose in chapter 5 exceeds what we can catch in secure facts. Rosa shares one of Faulkner's own fascinations, his attraction to in-between states, whether of light and time (twilight is his favored time for fiction, and "Twilight" was an early title for *The Sound and the Fury*), of mind, or of sexual ("androgynous") or racial identity. Hence her description of Clytie: *"paradox . . .—Clytie who in the very pigmentation of her flesh represented that debacle which had brought Judith and me to what we were and had made of her (Clytie) that which she declined to be just as she had declined to be that from which its purpose had been to emancipate her, as though presiding aloof upon the new, she deliberately remained to represent to us the threatful portent of the old"* (195).

To Rosa, Clytie's individuality is at war with her representativeness. Whites, especially whites who have little to do with blacks or with blacks as peers, often stick individual blacks with the burden of representing all blacks or black culture at large. Rosa does that to Clytie, but at the same time senses that the distinctness in Clytie's position, which makes it seem hybrid, makes it too complicated to be representative. To be sure, we all bear the burden of representation; any of us can be made to represent any number of grand historical forces. We might see Clytie's case as an ordinarily complex instance of the ways we all weave mundane compromises between the personal and the social, but Rosa sees it as special. She finds it strangely paradoxical that Clytie represents slavery and has been freed from slavery without having really been a slave, and that, as one of the newly empowered, Clytie presides over the new even while remaining a sign of the old. Though the mix of old and new is hardly so unusual, Rosa transmogrifies the ordinary mix into the transcendentally representative hybrid.

But Rosa sees even herself as a hybrid creature. When she recalls her fantasy of Bon and Judith's courtship, she calls herself

> *child enough not to need to hide, whose presence would have been no violation even though he sat with her, yet woman enough to have gone to her entitled to be received . . .—Yes, child enough to go to her and say 'Let me sleep with you'; woman enough to say 'Let us lie in bed together while you tell me what love is,' yet who did not do it because I should have had to say 'Dont talk to me of love but let me tell you, who know already more of love than you will ever know or need.' Then my father returned and came for me and took me home and I became again that nondescript too long a child and yet too short a woman.* (184–85)

The child-sophisticate, who feels more romantic and womanly than the older Judith, appears sexless and insignificant in other people's eyes, remaining subject to the call of Daddy and the stamp of childhood that his call carries with it. Some of this in-betweenness is no more than the usual medley of adolescence. But it is characteristic of Rosa, who in another typically Faulknerian conceit seems paradoxically frozen in the midst of motion: locked in the past but with no waning of energy in the present, and suspended for what feels like hours on the stairs that it takes her so many dense pages to mount (pp. 169–77, interrupted by a flashback and then resuming at p. 186).

Rosa's ironic distance redeems her from the suffocating closeness of her rhapsody and the ponderousness of her self-conscious paradoxes. It may help to call attention to her irony, because some readers get so distracted by her orotund grandiloquence that they miss the critical perspective she takes on her own wrenchings of language and emotion. She turns satirically to the lingo of allegory and mythology— Sutpen the demon and ogre, Clytie the Cerberus and sphinx—to mock her youthful melodramatics. At age 20 she tried out a more benign myth, converting Sutpen from an ogre and demon into a *"titan"* who might be *"receptive"* to *"that magic in unkin blood which we call by the pallid name of love"* (209), only to find she had to trade that fond belief for *"the death of hope and love, the death of pride and principle, and then the death of everything save the old outraged and aghast unbelieving which has lasted for forty-three years"* (210). That briefly recounted sequence in her own conception of Sutpen, from evil demon to potentially loving titan to something that she still leaves vague but at least to something else, shows that now, 43 years after the third of those stages begins, she can look back with enough critical distance to see the shifts and fits and starts, and dub herself *"self-mesmered fool"* (171, 174).

She focuses her critical energy and irony on her supposedly grand antagonist, Sutpen, and on herself. On others, especially on Clytie, she seems petrified in the delusions of her late adolescence now 43 years extended. Clytie has simply not been part of Rosa's calculus. She hurries out to the Sutpen place expecting Henry, and instead runs literally into Clytie, whom she introduces as the *"cold Cerberus"* of Sutpen's *"private hell"*—

> *the face without sex or age because it had never possessed either: the same sphinx face which she had been born with, which had looked down from the loft that night beside Judith's, and which she still wears now at seventy-four, looking at me with no change, no alteration in it at all, as though it had known to the second when I was to enter, had waited there during that entire twelve miles behind that walking mule and watched me draw nearer and nearer and enter the door at last as it had known (ay, perhaps decreed, since there is that justice whose Moloch's palate-paunch makes no distinction between gristle bone and tender flesh) that I should.* (169)

This is no description of Clytie, of a person (or a character—a fictional person). Here again Rosa sees not Clytie but instead some amalgam of her own purposes projected onto Clytie, sees what she fears from Clytie. She fears, in part—with an insight in the midst of her error—her very incapacity to see Clytie, so that she calls Clytie sexless, changeless, ageless, and a sphinx: archetype of the grandly foreign, the exotically meaningful but mysterious. It is true that we hear nothing of Clytie's sexuality, but we hear about her through characters who have no interest in it, and mostly through Rosa, who, fearful of arrest in her own sexuality, can find relief in projecting a halted eros onto someone else.

Clytie seems more intensely Rosa's rival once it turns out, here, that she is still alive, like Rosa stretching the novel's storied past into its storytelling present. Here, as in the only earlier scene with Clytie, the scene at the end of chapter 1 that Rosa now recalls, Clytie appears belatedly and as hanger-on to the characters Rosa prefers to see, Henry and Judith, Clytie's half-brother and half-sister. With her Sutpen face (33, 169), she looms more as a sign of Rosa's resentment for Sutpen's gruff sexuality than as someone Rosa can imagine having desires of her own. Instead, Rosa evades Clytie's immediacy by exoticizing her into a representative of oriental mysteries that would likely be farther from Clytie's knowledge than from Rosa's. And so Rosa teases herself (*"as though . . . , perhaps"*) with a vision of Clytie as some extrasensory harpy-demon who knows Rosa's thoughts and movements ahead of time and perhaps even decrees them. At last the momentum of that vision carries Rosa away to the point where, imagining justice as Moloch, she almost makes it sound as if Clytie, now transformed beyond recognition into some cruel and bloody arbiter of justice, is about to *eat* her.[6]

None of this has much to do with the slave-daughter of a Yoknapatawpha planter, though it tells something about the imagination of puritan Goodhue Coldfield's daughter. Child of a conscience-ridden man, Rosa is preoccupied with what other people see in her—hence her vision of Clytie watching her across 12 miles—or say about her. *"So they will have told you . . . ,"* she says in the first words of her monologue, and she repeats that remark—or its variants, *"they cannot have told you"* and so on—throughout the chapter, along with questions about *"who shall say"* (179) and about what people did (213) or didn't (175) see in her. And so to Rosa, Clytie's *"inscrutable coffee-*

colored face" depicts, in Rosa's own equation, not Clytie so much as Clytie's father, his *"clairvoyant will tempered to amoral evil's undeviating absolute"* (171). To Rosa's fantasy, Clytie becomes an almost abstract allegorical force, an omen of evil itself, and the projection of Rosa's own conscience-ridden fears about the forbidden things she desires from Sutpen.

She thus forgets about and, in a sense, cannot even see Clytie. When she first looks at Clytie's Sutpen face, she imagines it is Henry (169), which repeats the structure of that earlier scene where we first hear of Clytie. There, too, Rosa—and Faulkner—use the phrase "Sutpen face" as a feint to make us expect Henry before we discover it is Clytie. With dramatic indirectness, we discover the very existence of Clytie at the same time, made more poignant by her closeness to Judith—not exactly the usual pattern when a master had more than one set of children. Moreover, in the later scene, Clytie's face in the dark when Rosa expects Henry has an effect of usurpation, supplanting Rosa's fevered anticipation with Clytie's own calmer force.

After Rosa recognizes the face as Clytie's, she still hears something else when Clytie speaks. *"Dont you go up there,"* says Clytie, trying to stop Rosa beneath the stairs; and Rosa thinks, *"and again it was as though it had not been she who spoke but the house itself that said the words. . . . Yes, I stopped dead, no woman's hand, no negro's hand, but bitted bridle-curb to check and guide the furious and unbending will—I crying not to her, to it; speaking to it through the negro . . . , expecting and receiving no answer because we both knew it was not to her I spoke: 'Take your hand off me, nigger!' "* (172–73). Though it feels to Rosa as if Clytie is devoid of personal agency and transfigured into the house itself, Rosa presumes that she knows what Clytie the nonperson thinks. And surprise of surprises, she decides that Clytie thinks exactly what Rosa herself thinks, even to the point of returning the presumption by understanding Rosa's spiral of arcane fantasy about Clytie (*"we both knew it was not to her I spoke"*). When at last she speaks to Clytie, Rosa's quick harsh words, so antithetical to her whirl of abstract surmising, icily confirm how preposterous and even comical it is to suppose that Clytie, from such words, would ever anticipate the frenzy of Rosa's unspoken thoughts. For Rosa to presume she knows what Clytie thinks is therefore another way of failing to see Clytie at all and instead projecting onto Clytie some form of her own self. Later, in a softer memory of a less feverish time, she almost admits as much: *"We were . . . strangers. I do not know what Clytie thought"* (195).

With such tangles of presumption and abstraction, Rosa's style in chapter 5 writhes into some of American and modern fiction's most involuted and densely packed extravangances. The contortions of vocabulary and syntax ease off some after she finally reaches the top of the stairs (187), which contributes to the way her protracted exertions to get past Clytie and up those stairs start to sound comic even amidst all the grim anguish. Indeed, it can help perplexed or impatient readers to emphasize, as I have tried to here, the amusing side of Rosa's tortuous pathos. And Faulkner helps not only by softening the style about halfway through the chapter, after Rosa climbs the stairs, but also by pacing it with occasional short, punchier sentences, including the first sentence of over half the paragraphs (for example, "I got none" [173], "That was all" [187 and 199], "That was my courtship" [204]), which helps readers assess where they stand in Rosa's thicket of syntax. Meanwhile, the gnarled phrases, the furiously winding sentences and paragraphs, the striking neologisms, all evoke an old woman's wrought up fervor, defying stereotypes that can lead readers to expect dry frustration. Rosa often gives her neologisms and other words one last inch of intensity by adding a "y" that twists her nouns into adjectives: globy, massy, trashy, heady-perfect, flushy, nooky, moony, rubbishy, miragy, snarly. (Such words appear only a few times in the rest of the book.) Her eerie mix of self-satiric comedy with what she calls *"some cumulative over-reach of despair itself"* (174) finally aspires to the unpredictably circuitous and eerily vivid condition of dream.

Dream is Rosa's preferred state. She longs for what she calls *"that true wisdom which can comprehend that there is a might-have-been which is more than truth, from which the dreamer, waking, says not*

It's Just Incredible. It Just Does Not Explain

'Did I but dream?' but rather says, indicts high heaven's very self with: 'Why did I wake since waking I shall never sleep again?' " (177–78). It seems to Rosa that we get only one chance to dream, and once we waken, that chance is gone. Indeed, she moves directly from this anguished question to the fairy-tale memory of her own supposed one time, her *"summer of wistaria,"* as she wistfully calls it. *"Once there was—"* she begins, in her private equivalent of "Once upon a time." But with that she interrupts herself to remark the wistaria of this summer of 1909, and then to insist on the unwilled quality of memory, claiming that such things as the *"sense, sight, smell"* of wistaria are the *"substance of remembering,"* that memory is a function of the muscles, not the mind or brain, *"and its resultant sum is usually incorrect and false and worthy only of the name of dream."* Then she loops back, after some examples for Quentin's edification, to how *"Once there was (they cannot have told you this either) a summer of wistaria. It was a pervading everywhere of wistaria (I was fourteen then)."* This is the center of Rosa's chapter-long dithyramb, the center of her memory and longing, which she sees as all condensed into one summer of secret adolescent infatuation for Charles Bon, a man she never met or even saw. Thus her throb of horror, albeit five years later, when Wash Jones shouts in the street that "Henry has done shot that durn French feller," and her frenzied rush to the Sutpen house to charge up the stairs and find—she hardly knows what—Henry's explanation, perhaps, or Bon's body, or Judith's grief.

She finds none of those things, nor any substitute for them. She finds only blankness and anticlimax: *"That was all,"* she says. *"Or rather, not all, since there is no all, no finish; it not the blow we suffer from but the tedious repercussive anti-climax of it, the rubbishy aftermath"* (187) that extends into her silent toilsome life with Judith and Clytie on the crumbling plantation. The complication, then, comes because, despite her insistence that she can have only one chance for the dream that she sees as the center of her imagination and identity, she gets a second chance when Sutpen looks at her one afternoon and then announces (more or less) that they will marry.

Sutpen's advent in Rosa's love life might make us look skeptically at her romantic reverie of wistaria and dream, her sense that there can be only one chance or that a second chance is so remarkable. When, in the midst of introducing her fairy-tale memory of wistaria (which sometimes blooms twice) with the word "*Once*," she suddenly interrupts herself to observe that 1909 has brought another summer of wistaria, she unwittingly indicates that chances can recur summer after summer, that there is no mere *once*. Sure enough, not only the wistaria surges again in 1909. The passion of this very monologue implies that Rosa, named for a flower, herself blooms again, and thus that she has too narrowly defined what can lead to dream.

For in chapter 5 as in chapter 1, Rosa conceives women's sense of self entirely through their social and erotic relation to men. The dream at the center of her longing has room for nothing about her except her connection to men, even if the connection is as silly as her childhood crush on Bon or as ominous as her speechless submission to Sutpen (and for Rosa, speechlessness is a terrible sacrifice). But especially in chapter 5, the eloquence of this woman who lives by herself defies her own feelings about dependence on men, tugging at a thread in the routine ideological fabric of feminine submission. Without thinking about it, Rosa defies the notions about women and men that she unconsciously takes from the world around her. Yet even as she defies those notions, she carries them on.

And so she thinks flamboyantly that she can say to Sutpen: "*I hold no substance that will fit your dream but I can give you airy space and scope for your delirium*" (209–10). She sees her virtue as Sutpen's wife solely in how her blankness, now that she has lost her fourteen-year-old's dream of Bon, can leave more range for *his* dream. Rhetorically, she takes her self-denial as something grand.

Then suddenly the engagement collapses. She promises to tell why:

I will tell you what he did and let you be the judge. (Or try to tell you, because there are some things for which three words are three too many, and three thousand words that many words too less, and this is one of them. It can be told; I could take that many sentences, repeat the bold blank naked and outrageous words just as he spoke them, and bequeath you only that same aghast and outraged unbelief I knew when I comprehended what he meant; or take three thousand sentences and leave you only that Why? Why? and Why? that I have asked and listened to for almost fifty years.) (208)

She promises to tell why, but never does, though again chapter 5 seems not to represent exactly what she says to Quentin that afternoon. In any case, the partly comical disproportion between her promise to tell—whether in three words or three thousand sentences—and her "aghast and outraged unbelief" that it can be told provokes a curiosity that Faulkner teasingly refuses to satisfy. Apparently, Sutpen said some "bold blank naked and outrageous words" that she cannot comprehend the motive for and that somehow brought an end to things, but she doesn't say what words or how they brought an end. Whatever it was, it was quick: *"a certain segment of rotten mud walked into my life, spoke that to me which I had never heard before and never shall again, and then walked out; that was all"* (214). So much for her dream of giving airy space and scope for his delirium.

She blames her father, circuitously, by claiming that the town would say she blames him, and soon veering into terms so personal that they suggest her own feelings as well:

They will have told you: daughter of an embusqué [a shirker] *who had to turn to a demon, a villain: and therefore she had been right in hating her father since if he had not died in that attic she would not have had to go out there to find food and protection and shelter and . . . she would not have become engaged to him and if she had not become engaged to him she would not have had to lie at night asking herself Why and Why and Why as she has done for forty-three years: as if she had been instinctively right even as a child in hating her father and so these forty-three years of impotent and unbearable outrage were the revenge of some sophisticated and ironic sterile nature on her for having hated that which gave her life.* (212)

Psychoanalytically—which is to say, unconsciously—the daughter's hate for the father is a defense against her love for the father. Such love can grow more urgently defended against when the mother dies early and leaves the father to the daughter, thus threatening to fulfill the daughter's oedipal fantasy. The same oedipal structure seems reenacted in Rosa's attraction to the husband of her much older sister, the sister who, as rival for the father's affection, can substitute for the mother's role as rival. In such a context, when Goodhue Coldfield nails himself into the attic not long after his sister runs off and leaves him alone to a daughter careening into adolescence, he seems to shirk more than military duty, though we never hear much about his feelings for his daughter. Thus when Rosa says she hates "that which" gave her life, her impersonal pronouns hint at more than her father or mother. She also hates sexuality itself, which gave her life but which she feels as a threat because she cannot progress past the forbidden desire for her father and—much more so—the inevitable defense against that desire.

Hence she envisions sexuality as evil or corrupting, even when she insists, while recalling her crush on Charles Bon, that though *"no man had yet to look"* at her *"nor would ever—twice,"* she still desires men: *"But root and urge I do insist and claim, for had I not heired too from all the unsistered Eves since the Snake?"* (179). By tracing her desire to Eve she associates it with disobedience and evil. She describes her attraction to Sutpen as dirty, as *"deluded sewer-gush"* (204), and refers to the femininely sexual body, with a huff of disgust, as so much *"male-furrowed,"* *"mammalian,"* and *"ravening meat"* (181, 182, 204).

In discussing Rosa Coldfield or any other character psychologically, we risk attributing to that character a fuller history and personality than a character can have. A character is not the same as a person. There is no more to Rosa Coldfield than what appears in *Absalom, Absalom!*, whereas there is more to a person than turns up in any account of that person, which explains why the *kinds* of interests we take in people and in characters overlap and yet differ. A person, for example, could not speak an unspeakable monologue, as a character can. Characters can act in strange ways that people cannot, whereas people act, whether strangely or not, in a fuller context of personality than characters.

In discussing a character, then, such as Rosa Coldfield, whether in psychoanalytic terms or in any other terms of psychological realism, we risk attributing to her a fullness of personal history beyond what the text includes and so distorting her into something that loses the unrealistic oddity that helps make her so interesting. What balances that risk is that we might find some interest in how an author sees characters along lines similar to personalities. For even apart from any knowledge of Freud (Faulkner knew at least a little of Freud, though he liked to deny it), Faulkner tended to conceive characters in ways congruent with psychoanalytic patterns of interpretation. But not everything about them can be explained in psychoanalytic terms. There is no description in psychoanalysis for an afternoon of italics (though there may be descriptions for the motive to write that way). That is a textual phenomenon that signals something in excess of ordinary speech, and in excess of ordinary or systematic conceptions of personality.

Indeed, even at the level at which we might still try to discuss Rosa psychologically, she herself tries to see experience running in excess of systematic thought and breaking down conceptual patterns: *"Because there is something in the touch of flesh with flesh which abrogates, cuts sharp and straight across the devious intricate channels of decorous ordering, which enemies as well as lovers know because it makes them both:—touch and touch of that which is the citadel of the central I-Am's private own: not spirit, soul; the liquorish and ungirdled mind is anyone's to take in any darkened hallway of this earthly tenement. But let flesh touch with flesh, and watch the fall of all the eggshell shibboleth of caste and color too"* (173). She feels drawn to those moments when enemies and lovers clash, blend, and blur, rather than to the sorting of people and experience into falsely neat categories ("eggshell shibboleths") like class or race. At the same time, Rosa's determined insistence that her experience defies familiar categories can itself provoke interpretation and psychoanalytic readings, for it is not merely some philosophical preference. Rather, it seems motivated by a wish to escape from categories she feels herself falling into.

When Clytie puts her hand on Rosa to stop her from climbing the stairs, Rosa describes the two of them as *"joined by that hand and arm which held us, like a fierce rigid umbilical cord, twin sistered to the fell darkness which had produced her"* (173). If she imagines Clytie as her twin sister, then she imagines Sutpen as her father, which is part of what attracts him to her. She also imagines Sutpen as conceiving ("producing") Clytie in evil ("fell") darkness, plausibly enough, since we can hardly suppose his relation to Clytie's mother as anything but abusive. Still, Rosa tinges it with a sense that sex itself is an evil doing in the dark, one she feels both drawn to—provoking her identification with Clytie as twin sister—and repulsed by—provoking her disgust. Either way, she's curious, so that her most characteristic childhood activity is to listen through *"closed forbidden"* (180) doors, trying to learn about that world of secrets reserved for adults. Later, as an adult herself, she can never reach the other side of the door, never settle into a healthy adult sexuality. It is not just that she is afraid, though fear is part of it. She also lives in a time and place where, after the Civil War, women vastly outnumber men, so that history conspires with personality to isolate her. Southerners of Quentin's—and Faulkner's—generation grew up among women widowed or, like Rosa, left single by the war.

Rosa thus feels frozen in the lonely aftermath of her broken engagement 43 years before, when she was only 20. She would rather be frozen six years earlier in her summer of wistaria, when she was 14. Her infatuation then, or so she keeps insisting through her long, fervent rapture about adolescent passion, was not love: *"(I did not love him; how could I? I had never even heard his voice, had only Ellen's word for it that there was such a person)"* (181–82). And again: *"I did not love him. (How could I have, when I had never seen him?) And even if I did, not as women love, as Judith loved him. . . . If it was love (and I still say, How could it be?) it was the way that mothers love"* (182). And once more: *"I . . . , who did not love him in the sense we mean it because there is no love of that sort without hope; who (if it were love) loved with that sort beyond the compass of glib books: that love which gives up what it never had"* (185). She has enough self-understanding not to believe her own denials. She can hear the straining parenthesis, the tone of evasion and defense, and yet she can't help returning to deny again. She would rather see her desire as motherly, as not "in the sense we mean," than own up to it as erotic; and her denial fits the way her oedipal anxiety has made her imagine sex, especially with Sutpen, as forbidden and dirty.

Since outright denial feels unconvincing, she grasps after more roundabout ways to imagine that somehow her desire is not sexual. She claims repeatedly that she is only a child, trying to reassure herself that she is somehow presexual. More adventurously, in the rhetorical climax of her rapture over that summer of wistaria, she declares herself *"all polymath love's androgynous advocate"* (182). If she is androgynous, a man-woman, then she might have something other than a woman's ordinary desire, and so she hopes, unconsciously, to prop up her fiction that she escapes the contamination of lust. Through all these regressive fantasies, these claims that her love is not sexual and that she's only a child or that she's androgynous, Rosa fixes tremulously on her adolescent moment of transition to adult sexuality, straining to arrest or even reverse her development before it can lead to the yearnings she has come to feel as contaminating. But she cannot hover forever at 14 or at that still younger age that the anxieties of 14 make her yearn for nostalgically, and so, amid all these other claims, she also imagines, still more desperately, that she lived as a man and should have been a man.

Her fantasy is so unexpected and comes so much in the midst of her passionately tangled rhetoric that it has provoked hardly any comment from critics, but it is so extravagant and frank that it demands our attention:

> *That was the miscast summer of my barren youth which (for that short time, that short brief unreturning springtime of the female heart) I lived out not as a woman, a girl, but rather as the man which I perhaps should have been. I was fourteen then, fourteen in years*

ABSALOM, ABSALOM!

*if they could have been called years while in that unpaced corridor
which I called childhood, which was not living but rather some
projection of the lightless womb itself; I gestate and complete, not
aged, just overdue because of some caesarean lack, some cold head-
nuzzling forceps of the savage time which should have torn me free
. . . ; I like that blind subterranean fish, that insulated spark whose
origin the fish no longer remembers, which pulses and beats at its
crepuscular and lethargic tenement with the old unsleeping itch
which has no words to speak with other than 'This was called light,'
and that 'smell,' and that 'touch,' that other something which has
bequeathed not even name for sound of bee or bird . . . equipped
only with that cunning, that inverted canker-growth of solitude
which substitutes the omnivorous and unrational hearing-sense for
all the others. . . . But it was . . . no summer's caesarean lack which
should have torn me, dead flesh or even embryo, from the living: or
else, by friction's ravishing of the male-furrowed meat, also wea-
poned and panoplied as a man instead of hollow woman.* (179–81)

She connects the feeling that she lived as a man, and should have been
a man, to her barrenly youthful female heart, suggesting that she felt
inadequate as a woman and therefore that her reaching for manhood
comes less from a sense of masculine identity than from a sense of
feminine failure. For this interlude, at least, she extends her regressive
fantasy, her urge to escape adult failures, back beyond childhood and
all the way to envisioning herself as floating in the watery womb,
14 years overdue, with a ludicrous improbability that underlines the
desperate comedy of her fantasy. She thinks of herself there in the
womb as a blind fish, suggesting the (seemingly) sexless and primal, a
time in which, to paraphrase the way she amazingly puts it, sex hadn't
even a name, and suggesting also the squirmy, phallically male, which
fits her fantasy of manhood. Or perhaps more acutely, it fits her grasping after the fantasy of an alternative, any alternative, to the female
sexuality she fears she has failed at. Her only sense, she supposes, is
hearing, so that like a child she can listen to what she feels afraid and
unable to do herself.

In Faulkner's *Sanctuary*, Temple Drake has a similar but more
menacingly intense fantasy. She imagines that all of a sudden, with " 'a

80

kind of plopping sound,' " she transforms into a man, safe from the men who want to rape her.[7] Rosa fears sex for less practical and more elaborate reasons, but both she and Temple act out and defend against their fear with fantasies of sexual transformation.

Rosa can hardly sustain so farfetched a fantasy, but she can pretend to sustain it through her dreamy summer of romance and wistaria, because—with no one to tell about her feelings, no friend, sister, or brother, not even Bon himself, whom she never sees—there's no one to break the bubble of fantasy. But six years later, she cannot pretend that her desire for Sutpen has nothing of lust in it. She would rather be frozen in the fantasy of 14 that she nostalgically looks back to as presexual, but instead she has frozen in the afternoon of 20 when her engagement to Sutpen collapsed after he *"spoke the bald outrageous words."* She doesn't say what those words were, except that they were *"exactly as if he were consulting with Jones or with some other man about a bitch dog or a cow or mare"* (210). However abusive the words, his talking to her as if she were a bitch or cow or mare removes any possibility for imagining that her relation to him is free of lust or sex. Her self-described fixation on that moment indicates a sadly confused fascination with what she nevertheless finds frightful and repulsive. She wants to grow beyond it, but that would require her to sort out the adult sexuality—her own, not his—that she fears even more.

And yet, the sudden flurry of suspense at the end of chapter 5, when Rosa tells Quentin that "something" (216) is living at the Sutpen house, indicates that after all those years she is ready for something new. She wants Quentin to help, which now mysteriously seems to be the goal of all she has told him that afternoon. If the wistaria blooms a second time that summer (3), then it seems that Rosa, this woman named for a flower, is ready to bloom again with it.

QUESTIONS ABOUT PLOT, REVISITED

If we now return to the questions about plot that conclude the previous chapter, some answers have changed, and we have one major new question: 1) why does Sutpen go to New Orleans? 2) why does Henry vanish? 3) why does Henry kill Charles Bon? 4) why does Rosa not marry Sutpen? and 5) what is the "something" living in the Sutpen house? As we saw at the beginning of this chapter, nothing has changed for the first question, but Mr. Compson has presented a much needed answer for the second and third, an answer that Rosa seems to know nothing about. Even so, Mr. Compson himself admits that his explanation is "just incredible" and "just does not explain." Meanwhile, we still don't know why Rosa didn't marry Sutpen. She promises to tell, but before we hear any more than that it had to do with something crude he said, Rosa ends chapter 5 and the first half of the novel, more or less, with a new mystery—"There's something in that house" (216)—which gives us a new question to take into the chapters that follow.

6

An Awful Lot of Delayed Information: Chapters 6–7

NEW INFORMATION, NEW NARRATIVE STRUCTURE

"Am I going to have to hear it all again" (345), wonders the exhausted Quentin, in another of the innumerable small moments that represent the novel as a whole. In this instance, Faulkner uses the moment partly for some good-humored self-parody. As he presents Quentin's exhaustion, Faulkner sympathizes with the possibly weary readers who, like Quentin, must hear it all again, because chapters 6 and 7 go back over the plot repeated so many times in earlier chapters.

But the new chapters add a great deal of new information and interpretation, including new answers to the first four of the five questions about plot that we reviewed at the end of the previous chapter. It turns out that Rosa's engagement with Sutpen collapsed after he proposed that they have a child first and then marry only if the child is male (222, 348, 355). That adds little to our knowledge, though, since we already knew that the engagement collapsed when Sutpen said something offensive. The severest shift comes with the discovery that Charles Bon is Thomas Sutpen's son, which Faulkner renders through Shreve, Quentin's Canadian roommate at Harvard. First, Quentin tells Shreve some other new material, the story of how Sutpen coldly put aside and repudiated a wife and son in Haiti before coming to Yoknapatawpha. Then Shreve interrupts: " 'All right,' he said. 'So that Christmas Henry brought him home, into the house, and the demon looked up and saw the face he believed he had paid off and discharged twenty-eight years ago. Go on." "Yes," Quentin says, and then goes on as Shreve asks (331).

Shreve's role as ignorant outsider makes him the character most like the novel's readers. For the more ordinary character to reveal such information and reveal it in an impatient, let's-get-on-with-things way contrasts ironically with its startling effect on the story. Shreve means to push the story onward, but he forces on readers, as well as on himself and Quentin, a need not only to surge forward but also to reevaluate what we have already read or heard—a huge task, 70 percent of the way into the novel. Thus Quentin spends the next pages telling the same story over again from the perspective of this new information, which, for example, clarifies exactly what led Sutpen to the extraordinary length of traveling to New Orleans to investigate Bon (335), though we still do not know what he did there, whether he spoke to anyone or only made sure it was the same Charles Bon (333).

From this perspective, it no longer appears that Henry repudiates family and birthright because his father tells him on that Christmas Eve of 1860 that Henry's friend Bon is already married back in New Orleans. Nor does it any longer appear that Henry, after seeing the New Orleans wife, then kills Bon to save Judith from marrying a bigamist. Even Mr. Compson, who tells the bigamy story, has admitted that it is "just incredible" and "just does not explain," because a morganatic marriage to a slave hardly seems likely to bother a slave owner of Henry's upbringing and station. The new information therefore makes more sense of the story. It suggests that Sutpen doesn't warn Henry, that Christmas Eve, about bigamy—it now turns out that Sutpen is a bigamist himself, an extraordinary irony on Mr. Compson's elaborate story. Instead, Sutpen tells Henry that Bon is Sutpen's son, and therefore Henry kills Bon not to prevent bigamy but rather to prevent something much more threatening: incest. Because Bon is Judith's—and Henry's—half-brother.

But how does Quentin learn all this, and how is it that he now attributes to his father some of the new interpretation it prompts, even though his father has told the bigamy story? After completing the manuscript draft, Faulkner added the following crucial explanation,[1] which quickly follows Shreve's casual disclosure:

> "Your father," Shreve said. "He seems to have got an awful lot of delayed information awful quick, after having waited forty-five years. If he knew all this, what was his reason for telling you that the trouble between Henry and Bon was the octoroon woman?"
>
> "He didn't know it then. Grandfather didn't tell him all of it either, like Sutpen never told Grandfather quite all of it."
>
> "Then who did tell him?"
>
> "I did." Quentin did not move, did not look up while Shreve watched him. "The day after we—after that night when we—"
>
> "Oh," Shreve said. "After you and the old aunt. I see. Go on. And Father said—" (332)

"Oh," Shreve says, with that same casualness. Apparently Quentin has already told him things that never get directly into the novel, so that Shreve can turn away Quentin's explanation once he recognizes it as familiar. But what Shreve can brush aside still hits readers with the force of stupefying surprise. Quentin, hitherto a distant observer (even if not so distant as Shreve), has somehow leapt a barrier, transforming himself from an often passive and inattentive listener to an active discoverer. And the new information that Quentin discovers has led his father to replace his own story about the fear of bigamy with a new story about the fear of incest.

Moreover, even this revelation, in typically Faulknerian fashion, confounds us with another secret encompassing the secret it discloses. On the one hand, it reveals that Quentin himself has found out that Bon was Sutpen's son, and leaves it pretty clear that Quentin found that out when he went with Rosa to the crumbling Sutpen house, as promised at the end of chapter 5. On the other hand, here near the end of chapter 7 it presses our attention to a mystery that the novel has long traded on, namely, the mystery that chapters 1–5 make us expect the scene of Rosa and Quentin going to the Sutpen house, but the novel leaps right past it.

The whole novel pivots on the scene it skips. At the end of the hot Mississippi September first half of the novel, Rosa dramatically announces that "there's something in that house" (216), and we realize that her reason for haranguing Quentin all afternoon is to prepare him to drive her to the Sutpen house that night where she hopes to discover what that something is. Then suddenly, in chapter 6, instead of turning to the Sutpen house, Faulkner hurdles past four months and a thousand miles, landing Quentin in another year, state, and climate, and isolating him yet again with someone else to listen and talk to. This time it is someone his own age and in that sense more like him, and yet someone from another country and so less wrought up than Rosa or Quentin's father with wayward Sutpens and Compsons, Yoknapatawpha lore, and the post–Civil War South. As everything in the first half of the novel leads up to whatever Rosa and Quentin find out at the Sutpen house, so it gradually becomes apparent that everything in the cold January Massachusetts second half leads away from what Rosa and Quentin find, even though Faulkner jumps past the scene without telling us what happened.

In some respects, he makes us feel the missing scene all the more by, in effect, taunting us over our ignorance of a scene that must shape everything after it. He even starts to lead into it, for after beginning chapter 6 with the surprises of snow, someone named "Shreve," January, Cambridge, and Rosa's death, so that we think he has altogether deserted the scene he has led up to at the Sutpen house, he soon reverts back to that scene, following Rosa and Quentin as they drive out to the Sutpen place that September evening (219–21). But then suddenly he drops them before they reach the house and returns to Shreve, who simply reviews the story at large (221–27), thus frustrating the expectations Faulkner makes a point of raising. He raises them once more only to frustrate them yet again at the end of chapter 6, where again he starts to reveal what happened out at the Sutpen house, and then Shreve tells Quentin to wait and suddenly the chapter stops short.

Not till much further along, in the words between Shreve and Quentin (332) added late to the manuscript, does Faulkner refer directly to the scene he has vaulted over. And yet he mentions it in a way that taunts us still more with his refusal to tell what happened, for neither Quentin nor Shreve completes the crucial sentences: "that night when we—" says Quentin. "After you and the old aunt. I see," responds Shreve.[2] And so we still have no answer to the fifth of our four questions about plot: what is the "something" living in the Sutpen house? (Some readers assume that Clytie and perhaps Jim Bond are the "something" out there, but Rosa specifically denies that she means Clytie [216, 270].)

The information that Bon is Sutpen's son, even as Faulkner leaves unclear how Quentin finds it out, affects the novel's view of Bon's son, Charles Etienne Saint-Valery Bon, barely referred to and never named before chapter 6, and Bon's grandson, Jim Bond, an entirely new character.[3] Structurally, the second half of the novel gets more complicated, and the scene that introduces these new characters is more intricately layered than anything in the first five chapters, so that critics often misread it by attributing words or ideas to the wrong character, to a character from, so to speak, another layer.

For that reason, I have charted the layers in some detail (see the appendix). During at least one stage in composition, Faulkner even set the whole scene apart by wrapping it in one vast parenthesis, some 37 pages long.[4] For a stretch, before he begins the parenthesis, the chapter proceeds much like Rosa's not-quite-spoken italicized thoughts in chapter 5. Faulkner shifts into italics, which he introduces as Quentin's thoughts (227), curiously interrupted by Quentin remarking "Yes" out loud (232), as if in response to Shreve talking while Quentin thinks, and then concluding the italics when Quentin thinks about Judith buying a tombstone, which Shreve responds to. Shreve's direct response indicates that Quentin has been speaking aloud some version of what he thinks, just as Rosa speaks a version of her italicized words in chapter 5. At that point the long parenthesis begins, in which Shreve starts to tell a story he must have heard before, recounting a time when Quentin, Luster,[5] and Mr. Compson go quail hunting and pause before the Sutpen tombstones to wait out a rainstorm. But in mid-sentence, with no ripple in syntax, Faulkner switches from Shreve's spoken words to his own authorial or external rendering (234) of the same scene. Faulkner thus unravels a great many strands—Quentin's thoughts, his speech, Shreve's speech, and Faulkner's narrative—in a jumble and blur that suggests their overlap and simultaneity.

From there it gets only more complicated (see the appendix). For our purposes, the point is that Faulkner soon modulates out of his authorial voice and into Mr. Compson's. As in earlier chapters, Mr. Compson is perfectly willing to suppose and imagine "facts," and often brilliantly, but still on the wobbly base of fragmented evidence and his own preferences. Here, his story of Charles Etienne Saint-Valery Bon plaits together what General Compson saw with what the general and Mr. Compson each speculates. Eventually, things grow still more intricate as Quentin starts to find his father's version troublesome, so that the narrative interrupts Mr. Compson's tale with Quentin's thoughts (259–61), themselves an indecipherable mixture, half his own guess at what might have happened and half his more private impulse of opposition to his father.

Such layering leads to many high jinks of structure and perspective. Early in the passage, Mr. Compson, Quentin, and Luster find themselves caught in the rain. The two Compsons head for shelter among a clump of cedars not far from the Sutpen house. (Faulkner's own house had a clump of cedars nearby, and so do most large houses in his fiction.) As they pause to look back at Luster leading the horses around a rain-swollen ditch, Mr. Compson speaks first to Luster and then to Quentin: " 'Better get on out of the rain,' Mr. Compson said. 'He's not going to come within a hundred yards of those cedars anyway' " (235). His point is unintelligible until, 32 pages later, when readers are liable to have forgotten it, Shreve tells—or Quentin remembers—how Mr. Compson teased Luster, a little cruelly, over his superstitious fear of the Sutpen graves by the cedars. The two allusions to Mr. Compson's condescension to Luster frame the larger passage, like the framing parenthesis.

In the midst of that frame, Mr. Compson, standing near the tombstones safely rid of Luster, warmly challenges Quentin, father-to-son, to draw the Sutpen and Compson past into his own imaginative present: "'Who would have paid for them?' Mr. Compson said. Quentin could feel him looking at him. 'Think' " (238–39). Mr. Compson tries to pass on his own perspective to his son, but as in earlier chapters, Mr. Compson's more eager imagination comes distorted by some troubling presumptions, such as those that make him tell Quentin not to worry about Luster getting soaked in the rain. His very need to distract Quentin's concern for Luster defines a gap in imaginative sympathy between the father and the son, even if the father has other advantages of knowledge and raconteur's zeal.

When Quentin suggests that Judith must have paid for the tombstones, Mr. Compson says, "Yes. They lead beautiful lives—women. Lives not only divorced from, but irrevocably excommunicated from, all reality" (240). It is hard to decipher how such assumptions, familiar from earlier in the novel, shape the tale Mr. Compson goes on to tell, which describes two determined women who lead anything but beautiful or disconnected lives. Clytie and Judith take on traditionally men's as well as traditionally women's responsibilities, and do so partly to care for a foolishly self-destructive man, Bon's son.

Mr. Compson's story of Bon's wife and son seems as suspect as his story of Clytie and Judith. To him, the woman from New Orleans is "the octoroon," perhaps an accurate way to refer to her, but also a reference laced with bias. Accurate because, in repeating what Grandfather Compson saw, he works from something more concrete than the only evidence he mentioned before, the picture on Bon's body—especially since Faulkner never explains how Mr. Compson knows about the picture, if indeed he does know about it and isn't just guessing from Grandfather's story about the woman who visits Bon's grave years later. But the expression "the octoroon" also suggests a bias, because the whole process of identifying her simply as *the* octoroon dissolves her individual identity into a racial category.

Mr. Compson's utter disinterest in the individuality of Bon's wife allows him to shape her according to his own leanings. He aestheticizes her, just as in chapter 4 he aestheticizes her master and husband. "It must have resembled," says Mr. Compson, in his evasive way of saying that he likes to imagine it resembled:

> a garden scene by the Irish poet, Wilde . . . ; the magnolia-faced woman a little plumper now, a woman created of by and for darkness whom the artist Beardsley might have dressed, in a soft flowing gown designed not to infer bereavement or widowhood but to dress some interlude of slumbrous and fatal insatiation, of passionate and inexorable hunger of the flesh, walking beneath a lace parasol and followed by a bright gigantic negress carrying a silk cushion and leading by the hand the little boy whom Beardsley might not only have dressed but drawn—a thin delicate child with a smooth ivory sexless face who . . . , breathing for air the milk-like and absolutely physical lambence which his mother's days and hours emanated, had seen little enough of sunlight before, let alone out-of-doors. (241–42)

Wilde and Beardsley evoke the decadence of Mr. Compson's fin de siècle 1890s rather than anything General Compson could think when he saw the graveyard in 1870, the same graveyard, now overgrown, where Mr. Compson embellishes the general's story for Quentin. The homosexual and eerily erotic ambiance suggested by Wilde and especially by Beardsley's drawings, often imitated in Faulkner's drawings, matches Mr. Compson's eagerly hinted view of the attraction between Henry and Bon in chapter 4 (for example, on pp. 119 and 148). For Mr. Compson, the focus is bodily and erotic. Where someone else might see a woman chafing under sexual slavery, he delights in imagining her as wholly absorbed by what has enslaved her, her very clothes the tools of someone else's "hunger" and "insatiation," as if her whole identity were distilled into the erotic and "absolutely physical" purposes she has been appropriated for. He sees those purposes not as "fatal" to her, their victim. Instead, he uncritically—with no sense of any issue at stake—adopts the slaveholder's view, falling back on the stereotype to see her as the femme fatale who victimizes Bon, as if Bon didn't choose, buy, and use her.

Perhaps building on something his father mentioned, Mr. Compson sharpens the scene visually by juxtaposing the decadent, half-pampered, and half-abused elegance of Bon's wife against the heavier corporeality—at least in his eyes—of her servant, a "bright gigantic negress." His resort to the feminine suffix ("ess") calls more attention to her, intensifying his array of cliché oppositions between servant and mistress, large and delicate, gaudy ("bright") and "soft," black and white. He turns to a grosser version of the same bigoted clichés in his tale of the delicate Charles Etienne Saint-Valery Bon and his wife, whom Mr. Compson introduces as a "coal black and ape-like woman" (257), as if her blackness and her stupidity had anything to do with each other. He refers to the "ape-like body of his [Saint-Valery Bon's] charcoal companion," supposes that young Bon "kenneled her with a gesture perhaps," and calls her "the black gargoyle" who resembled "something in a zoo" (258, 259, 262). All this suggests Mr. Compson's arch and sometimes callous posing at least as much as it gives any account of what went on among the Sutpens.

When Mr. Compson contrasts young Bon to the supposedly coarser people around him, he portrays him according to a particular style, the so-called decadent mannerism of turn-of-the-century aestheticism.[6] He sees Etienne (if, for clarity, we can refer to him by that name) as a "delicate child with a smooth ivory sexless face," one of Beardsley's androgynes, the unworldly product of a den set aside for effete pleasures. To Mr. Compson's mind, this offspring of decadent, cloistered eroticism must be outlandish even to himself and must yearn tragically to be ordinary. From a world so hermetically feminine, "breathing for air the milk-like ... lambence which his mother's days and hours emanated," he could not, to Mr. Compson, be truly male himself. And so Mr. Compson describes him as "talonless and fangless" (248), the "boy with his light bones and womanish hands" (250), and the "man with body and limbs almost as light and delicate as a girl's" (258).

Even as he describes Etienne's mother, Mr. Compson—attributing the thought to General Compson—admits parenthetically that he has no interest in her: "(your grandfather said you did not wonder what had become of the mother, you did not even care: death or elopement or marriage: who would not grow from one metamorphosis—dissolution or adultery—to the next carrying along with her all the accumulated rubbish-years which we call memory, the recognisable *I*, but changing from phase to phase as the butterfly changes once the cocoon is cleared, carrying nothing of what was into what is, leaving nothing of what is behind but eliding complete and intact and unresisting into the next avatar)" (245–46). Grandfather and Mr. Compson aestheticize Etienne's mother. They have no evidence to see her as oblivious to the past or future, the obsessive concerns of everyone else in *Absalom, Absalom!* Only one of them has seen her, and neither has spoken with her. They imagine her only as an artfully painted object and a tool of Bon's pleasure, and so they seize upon the flimsy supposition that she is somehow empty because it helps them repress the social fears that keep them from imagining anything more to her. She does not grow or remember, for Grandfather and Mr. Compson, because their social preconceptions make them incapable of imagining her growth and threatened by her memory, which might implicate people like themselves.

At another point, in a later year (how much later is not clear), but told to us earlier in the novel, Mr. Compson describes the same woman much more sympathetically as the "apotheosis of two doomed races presided over by its victim—a woman with a face like a tragic magnolia, the eternal female, the eternal Who-suffers" (141). In this other vision of Mr. Compson's, she is victim rather than femme fatale or victimizer. And rather than moving along oblivious to past and future, she suffers tragically and eternally. These opposite visions of the same woman are nevertheless alike in that both foist upon her a burden of extravagant *otherness*. They picture her as the human exotica against which Mr. Compson, who is so much more privileged but still has his educated burden of nervous restlessness, can shore up his sense of his own normalcy. It is equally convenient to find an "other" at either extreme. In one view, she is too oblivious for any political, cultural, or even erotic consciousness, which reinforces Mr. Compson's sense of his own privileged depth of consciousness. And in the other view, all by herself she can represent all suffering and thus mythologize victimization in a way that seems to hold it beyond what anyone else could have some role in or responsibility for.

It could seem that this is to read Mr. Compson too psychologically for a character whose life we hear so little about. But my focus has been on his process of evasion, repression, or displacement rather than on anything particular that he evades, and that pattern shows especially in the way he talks of Charles Bon's wife and child. The process of encumbering other people with burdens of representativeness, especially the process of white people loading individual black people with the burden of representing this or that principle or of representing black people in general, is one of the central concerns of Faulkner's *Light in August*. In that novel, Faulkner describes the way whites respond to Joe Christmas, a more or less white-looking character who supposes he might have some black ancestry. Joe is given and sometimes takes on—and sometimes defies—the role of black man not because he is or is not black, since we never know about that, but because people choose to see him in relation to what they decide are black roles. The core of mystery thus allows Faulkner to use people's responses to Joe, and the way their responses condition Joe's own anguished sense of identity, to explode the whole idea that there is some essential racial selfhood that necessarily has a particular meaning, as opposed to the meanings we often impose upon it.

Light in August is the model for this part of *Absalom, Absalom!*, in that young Etienne Bon's anguish, at least as Mr. Compson describes it, is the story of Joe Christmas all over again. In their childhood, women give them secret gifts of food (as Clytie does, 244), as if something is wrong with them that cannot be addressed openly. Both study their visage in a broken mirror that suggests their bifurcated identities (250). Both grow into silent, brooding, violent adults who fight pointlessly and furiously against whole groups of blacks. They take up with dark black, stupid women whom they apparently seek out as walking confirmations of white racism. They both seek escape through travel, and as they travel they fight alternately with blacks and whites, with anyone who accepts the dare to doubt that Christmas or Bon is black. They both settle in a run-down slave cabin where Bon's wife bears a son, and where a woman in *Light in August* bears a son that some people imagine is Christmas's. And both are likened, half-ironically and half-tragically, to Christ (261–62). Some of all this torment over Etienne Bon's racial identity comes with the authority of Grandfather Compson's observation, whereas some—the broken mirror, the analogy to Christ, and perhaps more—Mr. Compson fills in. Still, in this case he works from a grounding in reported fact. Young Bon, like Joe Christmas, is victim of a race prejudice he sometimes fights against with pride, but more often and more deeply internalizes, because he lacks any model of opposition to it.

If Mr. Compson depicts Etienne's mother by dissolving her individuality into racial and social category, then that is exactly what the stories of Etienne Bon and Joe Christmas expose as confining and cruel. Thus even when there is too little of a character's life to see far into any private history of motive, we can still discern the outer shapes of motive as they distort and embellish a story. In Mr. Compson's case, we can observe his inclination to see women and blacks as simpler than white men and his urge to exoticize and aestheticize. We can observe his fascination with the supposedly refined anxieties of the privileged and his presumption that people who lack his assurance of racial identity will undergo a frenzy of nervous suffering. Mr. Compson and indeed Faulkner himself fasten upon uncertain racial ancestry, in the person of Etienne Bon, as if it were exotically and fantastically tragic, rather than the ordinary circumstance of countless millions.

Still, that ordinary circumstance, though not in itself tragic, can be laden with tragedy by the meanings that people like Mr. Compson impose upon it.

When his story reaches young Bon's return to the Sutpen house after a year spent furiously trying to travel himself out of anguish, Mr. Compson suddenly declines to guess or make up what he doesn't know: "And nobody to know what transpired that evening between him and Judith." At that point, where Mr. Compson uncharacteristically balks, explaining *"Because there was love"* (259), his son, whom we have still heard so little from (though more in this chapter), uncharacteristically takes over and imagines a scene between young Bon and Judith. Quentin seems willing to linger in imagination of love, while his father apparently feels that such frankness would jeopardize the emotional evasions of his aesthetic distance.

Quentin concludes his scene by imagining that Judith says to young Bon *"Call me Aunt Judith, Charles"* (261). The structure of such a moment points intensely at the novel's complex layering. Quentin imagines Judith speaking those words, but never learns whether Judith or young Bon knows that she is his aunt after all, at least his half-aunt. Nor is there any indication that the elder Bon ever knows or does not know that Sutpen is his father and Judith his half-sister. Moreover, as Quentin sits in his dorm room and imagines this scene, he knows that Judith is young Bon's half aunt, but first-time readers of *Absalom, Absalom!* do not know that until late into the next chapter. Judith's words have vastly different meaning according to whether she knows her relation to Etienne and he doesn't, or he knows and she doesn't, or neither or both of them know, and according to whether readers know, at that point, that Quentin knows. In a history, a single set of facts might underlie all those possibilities, but here in a novel, the assorted permutations float together on more or less equal terms, though shifting somewhat between a first reading and a rereading.

Many critics of *Absalom, Absalom!* seem oblivious to such complexities. They routinely refer to characters and events as if, for example, the conversation between Judith and Etienne takes place in the same way that the conversations between Quentin and Shreve or Quentin and his father take place. They assume that Bon knows about his father or that Judith does not know that Bon is her brother, and then discuss how Bon or Judith responds to that knowledge or ignorance. That is to treat this novel as if it were a history, and so to cleanse away much of what makes *Absalom, Absalom!* special, even among other novels. Our ignorance and knowledge about who knows what, and the shifts in our knowledge as we read along, are themselves the plot of *Absalom, Absalom!* as much as the speculated actions of the characters. In this novel, plot is an act of mind. When critics say that Charles Bon does this or Sutpen does that, in instances where someone only supposes that Sutpen or Bon *might* have done this or that, then they describe as an action of Sutpen or Bon what in some sense is more truly an action of the character who does the speculating. The things that the Bons or Sutpens might have done are only selections from a vast spectrum of possibilities, but the characters who guess about them do so with a definiteness that distinguishes their guessing from almost any acts we hear about by the Bons or Sutpens. We cannot tell about the actions they guess at, but the guesses themselves are the main thing we're sure of.

The shifting recipe of guess and knowledge makes *Absalom, Absalom!* an intensely different book on rereading, when we see even the earlier parts through the lens of later knowledge. That leads to a series of extraordinary ironies, such as when we look back and see that Quentin imagines Judith telling Etienne Bon to call her Aunt Judith, before we know that she is indeed his aunt, and yet after Quentin knows. In chapter 1, for example, Rosa refers to Sutpen, in the passage we studied to open our reading of the novel, as that man "who had created two children not only to destroy one another and his own line . . ." (18). Rosa little suspects how much more meaning her words have than she intends. Not only do the two children she refers to, Henry and Judith, figuratively destroy each other when Henry murders Judith's fiancé and then vanishes, but unbeknownst to Rosa, Henry's murder also destroys another child of Sutpen, and not just figuratively.

Later, when Mr. Compson describes how Ellen, Judith, and Rosa concoct elaborate hopes for Bon while hardly even knowing him, he describes Bon as "a phantom: something which they engendered and created whole themselves; some effluvium of Sutpen blood and character, as though as a man he did not exist at all" (128). Little does he know, at that point, how literally Bon is indeed the creation of Sutpen blood and character. Still later, as Mr. Compson tries to explain what he believes must have been Henry's objection to Bon's concubine-wife, he explains that "that may have been the trouble with Henry— . . . not the fact that Bon's intention was to commit bigamy but that it apparently was to make his (Henry's) sister a sort of junior partner in a harem" (147). Mr. Compson insists that he means *Henry's* sister, but once we learn that Bon is Sutpen's son, his words start to mean *Bon's* sister as well, so that the need for parenthetical clarification takes on extra ironic force.

Such examples could be multiplied many times. Faulkner plays with his narrative so that the same words mean different things from different perspectives, and mean far more than the characters who speak them can intend. Mr. Compson supposes that Sutpen objected to his daughter's marriage because the man she sought to marry was in a sense already married, but it ironically turns out that Sutpen himself was already married when he married Judith's mother. All these ironies grow out of the hindsight produced by chapter 7, where at last we learn more than a whiff of rumor about Thomas Sutpen, the character whom the rest of the novel has so intensely focused on even as he remained a mystery.

A LIFE OF THOMAS SUTPEN

Chapter 7 at last recounts the life of Thomas Sutpen, which another novelist, beginning at the earliest point of the story, might have started with. It gives Sutpen's own version of his life, or more precisely,

Quentin's version of Mr. Compson's version of Grandfather Compson's version of Sutpen's version.

Grandfather announces that Sutpen's "trouble was innocence" (274), a showy claim, since it has so little to do with what anyone would associate with the brutal and secretive Sutpen. Grandfather's claim, oft repeated, is half dare and half tease, because he uses the word "innocence" in what logicians call an *equivocation*. That is, he deceptively connects unrelated ideas by using one word that has two unrelated meanings. Ostensibly, by "innocence" Grandfather means ignorant naiveté, since his point is that Sutpen's problem was ignorance of the world's ways. But he so insists on his claim for Sutpen's innocence that it starts to take on the additional sense of guiltlessness and childish purity, an implication that can only provoke us. To the extent that Sutpen represents the abuses of concentrated power or even the plantation system itself, Grandfather's playful insistence on Sutpen's innocence has the ring of one privileged man's apology for another and the danger of appealing to the many readers who have been taken in by the romantic myth of a lost plantation paradise. Today we connect that myth to *Gone with the Wind* (published the same year as *Absalom, Absalom!*) and its movie, but it was invented and made familiar before Margaret Mitchell's tearjerker by crassly racist popular novelists from the turn of the century like Thomas Nelson Page and Thomas Dixon, who nostalgically longed for return to a happy South that never existed. Indeed, some of my students find that myth so prevalent in the context they bring to *Absalom, Absalom!* that it helps to suggest that Faulkner tries to make his novel, in effect, an anti–*Gone with the Wind,* tries perhaps with a few fits and starts, for surely his horror at the myth comes mixed with a fascination that drives him to challenge it on so grand a scale.

By turning to the story of Sutpen's childhood, when he is liable to appear more sympathetic, Sutpen—and Grandfather and Mr. Compson—trade on their listeners' romantic sensibilities, as Faulkner does also, except to the extent that Faulkner can expect some readers to respond with more critical suspicion. Sutpen explains himself by what he calls the "boy-symbol," a term that caters to a narrow but familiar kind of literary critical interpreting. For many readers, symbols have been so exalted as the machine of understanding that they seize upon Sutpen's expression with a sense of relief. In the overly simple kind of literary criticism that often stands out among the methods many readers have encountered, it sometimes seems that the goal is to find a symbol, which is confining enough, but it can also seem that once the symbol is found then the critical act is over. Though that may still be the stuff of some English courses, it is antithetical to the tradition of symbol in so-called classic American literature.

In such works as Hawthorne's *The Scarlet Letter* or Melville's *Moby-Dick,* the symbol is anything but the key to confident understanding, because there is no confident or one-to-one relation between the symbol and anything it might symbolize. On the contrary, in a way that anticipates the structuralist linguistics of Ferdinand de Saussure, which have had so much influence on recent literary critical theory, the symbols of the scarlet letter or the white whale defy understanding by their anarchic capacity to represent so many different and even contradictory things. Not that anything goes, but that so many things go that they can shatter or at least complicate our capacity to isolate single meanings. Even so there remains, among many teachers, students, and critics, and sometimes among any of us, an impulse to resist the capacity for a novel like *Absalom, Absalom!* to sustain its elaborate uncertainties. That impulse makes us seek out symbols as the enforcers of certainty. We all need some certainty, and there will always be those who feel more comfortable with certainties than with mystery and enigma. It is no coincidence, then, that Sutpen decides he can explain his life by a single incident and a single symbol, for it suggests his need or yearning for certainties.

But it doesn't work. The "boy-symbol" explains that Sutpen's furious ambition derives from the incident when the ragged young Sutpen goes to deliver a message from his father to the plantation owner, and a house slave turns him away from the front door. That contradicts Sutpen's own story. According to him, he struck the idea of going to the West Indies to get rich before he ever went to the plantation door, when he heard his teacher read about the wealth of the islands. He waylaid the teacher to ask if it were true, and the furthest reach of his imagination was so feeble that when the teacher asked "Why not? . . . Didn't you hear me read it from the book?" he responded, "How do I know that what you read was in the book?" (302–3). Thus Sutpen's ambition predates the boy-symbol incident and takes its shape from a peculiarly unimaginative apprehension of the world around him. We can understand him better, then, if we do not limit ourselves to his own understanding of himself.

According to his own understanding, "All of a sudden he discovered . . . what he just had to do. . . . At the very moment when he discovered what it was, he found out that this was the last thing in the world he was equipped to do because he not only had not known that he would have to do this, he did not even know that it existed . . . until he was almost fourteen years old. Because he was born in West Virginia, in the mountains where—" (274–75). At that point, Shreve interrupts, observing that there was no West Virginia when Sutpen was born. If Quentin can get such matters wrong, that might raise our suspicion about how reliable the whole tale is. Similarly, Sutpen claims that while growing up in the woods, "he had never even heard of, never imagined, a place, a land divided neatly up and actually owned by men who did nothing but ride over it on fine horses or sit in fine clothes on the galleries of big houses while other people worked for them" (276). Ideas like Sutpen's "all of a sudden," "the very moment," and "never even heard of" have the convenience of simple and improbable certainty.

Sutpen himself describes feelings and observations that undermine his belatedly constructed certainties:

When he was a child he didn't listen to the vague and cloudy tales of Tidewater splendor that penetrated even his mountains because then he could not understand what the people meant, and when he became a boy he didn't listen to them because there was nothing in

sight to compare and gauge the tales by and so give the words life
and meaning, and no chance that he ever would (certainly no belief
or thought that someday he might), and because he was too busy
doing the things that boys do; and when he got to be a youth and
curiosity itself exhumed the tales which he did not know he had
heard and speculated about them, he was interested and would have
liked to see the places once, but without envy or regret. (277)

Sutpen is supposedly the source for this information about what he
didn't listen to, which suggests that "not listening" has become a
metaphor for a different kind of listening that includes a repression
rather than an absence of thought about what he listens to. In the
same manner, in *Light in August* (to name a memorable example of
something Faulkner does in many works), Faulkner sometimes introduces a character's half-conscious thoughts by saying that "he was not
thinking" those thoughts, and then going on to give the unthought
thoughts anyway, sometimes in italics.[7] For Sutpen the progression
moves steadily from "couldn't understand" to "couldn't give meaning," from "no chance that he would" to "no belief that he might,"
and then to actual curiosity and speculation, all before—if we accept
his earlier word—he knew that it existed at all.

After he comes down from the mountains, but still long before he
is turned away from the plantation door, he takes note of "niggers
working in the fields while white men sat fine horses and watched
them, and more fine horses and men in fine clothes, with a different
look in the face from mountain men about the taverns where the old
man was not even allowed to come in by the front door" (281). That
includes all the divisions of race and class that he says he never heard
of or imagined before he himself is turned away from the door. "He
had learned the difference not only between white men and black ones,
but he was learning that there was a difference between white men and
white men not to be measured by lifting anvils or gouging eyes or how
much whiskey you could drink then get up and walk out of the room.
That is," Quentin adds, "he had begun to discern that without being
aware of it yet" (282). The boy-symbol incident, therefore, exposes

young Sutpen to things he has already seen. It fixes in his memory in part because it points directly at him, but also because, although the class distinctions it enforces are far from new, at age thirteen or fourteen he is newly ready to question them. The boy-symbol thus crystallizes an awareness that has been growing for a long time. By focusing or at least trying to focus on the one incident, Sutpen defensively simplifies a feeling too complicated and threatening for him to understand.

He seems threatened, like all of us at times, and like readers who clutch at the boy-symbol for explanation, by exactly that possibility that he might not understand. When he describes his ambition as, "not what he wanted to do but what he just had to do whether he wanted to or not" (274–75), he exposes his desire as outside his control. "Because if he did not do it he knew that he could never live with himself for the rest of his life, never live with what all the men and women that had died to make him had left inside of him for him to pass on, with all the dead ones waiting and watching to see if he was going to do it right" (275). That suggests a sense of guilt, a fearful measuring of himself against an image of rightness and parental approval. Such fear is a normal part of growing up, although Sutpen also mentions, in a casual parenthesis, "something to Grandfather about his mother dying about that time" (278). The casualness expresses a need to make light of a loss that prompts at least some amount of irrational guilt in anyone, as Freud discusses in his essay "Mourning and Melancholia." His casualness defends against the pressure to live up to what he believes the "men and women who had died to make him" would want, an impossible task, and so a guilt-producing task that both drives our ambitions and makes it comforting to suppose, as Sutpen does, that the ambitions appear all of a sudden without any compromising history to them. And so he thinks of his family's movement from the mountains to the Piedmont plantation as "automotivation. . . . He didn't know why they moved, or didn't remember the reason if he ever knew" (278). If we forget the reasons we act, then we might imagine we can escape the expectation to live up to them. Vague as those reasons here remain, they indicate a web of personal, familial, and social motive far too complex for the boy-symbol and its one sudden moment to account for.

Sutpen almost admits as much to General Compson when nearly 20 years later, bereft of his youthful confidence, he returns to his story,

> telling Grandfather that the boy-symbol at the door wasn't it because the boy-symbol was just the figment of the amazed and desperate child; that now he would take that boy in where he would never again need to stand on the outside of a white door and knock at it: and not at all for mere shelter but so that that boy, that whatever nameless stranger, could shut that door himself forever behind him on all that he had ever known, and look ahead along the still undivulged light rays in which his descendants . . . waited to be born without even having to know that they had once been riven forever free from brutehood. (325–26)

Here, as Sutpen concedes that the story he used to explain his past cannot explain it, he betrays his confused motives. His concern for the boy-symbol comes less from the sympathy for poverty we might expect than from shame at it. He holds the boy-symbol in mind not to memorialize lower-class strife but instead to help the lower-class boys who follow him erase it from memory, as if it not only marked their suffering but also put them at fault for it.

His rhetoric about how he "would" take that boy in sounds hollow, for when given the chance to take in Wash Jones or Charles Bon he turns them away, though he doesn't exactly put it like that when, a little later, he describes Bon's arrival to General Compson. Bon is, nevertheless, his own descendant who "waited to be born" when young Thomas was turned away from the plantation door. Sutpen, as he tells General Compson, "stood there at his own door, just as he had imagined, planned, designed, and sure enough after fifty years the forlorn nameless and homeless lost child came to knock at it and no monkey-dressed nigger anywhere under the sun to come to the door and order the child away" (333). The distinction is deceptively fine. No slave comes to order Bon away, but Sutpen himself asks Henry, if not to order him away, then at least somehow to get rid of him. And Sutpen turns to Henry apparently without speaking for himself to his own son Bon, so that the snub seems colder and more deliberate than the slave's impersonal request, decades before, that the young Sutpen go around to the back door.

Bon, to be sure, doesn't come to the door in ragged poverty. But Wash Jones does, and he gets turned away, sometimes even by a slave, Clytie (155, 166, 229–30, 351). That shows the emptiness in Sutpen's self-serving remarks about what he "would" do. The snub to Wash comes back to haunt Sutpen when finally, after Sutpen's insult to Milly, Wash can take no more and kills him, which recalls how Sutpen, after getting turned away from the door, thinks about killing the plantation owner (292–96). Mr. Compson imagines that Wash sees Sutpen as an apotheosis of Wash himself. That thought seems more plausible from Mr. Compson than from Wash, because Mr. Compson knows, as Wash perhaps does not, that Sutpen began life in the same uneducated, "white trash" poverty that Wash lives in.

Knowingly or not, Sutpen seems to have picked out Wash exactly to represent Sutpen's own past, to keep it visibly before him. Indeed, Sutpen is the creature of his past much more elaborately than the boy-symbol alone can indicate. When he gets rebuffed at the door, he wonders how to combat the people who can turn him away, and decides that "to combat them you have got to have what they have that made them do what he did" (297). But that makes no sense, because if it makes them do what offends him, then once he has it too, instead of allowing him to combat them it will make him do the same offensive thing. Which is exactly what happens. Sutpen sets out to acquire what "they have," and once he gets it he turns away Charles Bon and Wash Jones exactly as the plantation owner had turned away Sutpen. Moreover, as he sets out to gain what the plantation owner had, he does so—consciously or not—with an appalling literalness. He remembers his childhood terror when the wealthy folks' carriage raced by, assuming the right to drive him and his sister off the road (288).

Later, wealthy himself, he races his own carriage, terrorizing his neighbors. As a boy, before he is turned away from the door and supposedly before he is aware of class and racial divisions, "he would creep up among the tangled shrubbery of the lawn and lie hidden and watch the man" who "lived in the biggest house he had ever seen and spent most of the afternoon . . . in a barrel stave hammock between two trees, with his shoes off and a nigger who wore every day better clothes than he or his father and sisters had ever owned and ever expected to, who did nothing else but fan him and bring him drinks" (284). Later, when Sutpen lives in the biggest house in Yoknapatawpha, instead of going to church he observes a more personal ritual. He spends Sunday afternoons reenacting and inverting his past, lying in a barrel stave hammock and drinking, with Wash Jones instead of a slave to serve the drinks, so that as he regales in his transformation to plantation grandee he can see before him a grown-up version of the ragged and illiterate young Sutpen who watched hidden from the shrubbery.

It is easy to miss the connection between the scenes of Sutpen drinking with Wash and the scene of Sutpen's childhood that they repeat, because we do not learn about the childhood scene (284) until, for the most part, after we hear in scattered fashion (27, 155, 230, 234, 344, 351–52) about the scenes with Wash that take place later. The gap in narrative that obscures such connections mimics the gap in Sutpen's own consciousness, given that we never learn whether he realizes how extraordinarily he is driven to repeat this one childhood scene of voyeuristic fascination. In a sense, then, Sutpen needs to have Jones turned away from the door to complete the picture. And he needs also, in the last irony of revenge, to turn away Bon, whose very name suggests that Sutpen chooses to marry a woman whose name recalls the plantation owner from Sutpen's childhood: Pettibone (289). (The genealogy at the end of the novel lists Bon as the name of Charles Bon's mother, which undermines Mr. Compson's already implausible notion [331] that Sutpen selects the name Bon for his son.) When something unravels Sutpen's first marriage, which had seemed to transform him into the plantation owner of his youth, he starts over again. But when that first marriage returns in the person of Charles Bon and he rejects it once more, he in effect rejects himself, turning away his own son, the new version of himself that he had committed himself to save from ever being turned away.

Instead of fighting the system that insulted him, Sutpen joins it. Instead of treating others with the respect he was denied, he enslaves others. To be sure, he had never questioned black slavery. Like Wash Jones, he looks at blacks with the hateful desperation of the downtrodden who bolster their self-esteem by abusing the yet more downtrodden. Hence Sutpen's irritation that some black slaves are better clothed and fed than he is. He also enslaves the white architect, which may seem no worse to us than enslaving blacks but lies flagrantly outside the ways of Sutpen's slaveholding world.

Curiously, Sutpen tells General Compson his story about the boy-symbol and about subduing the Haitian slave revolt not because he feels any need to explain himself—"he was not talking about himself. He was telling a story" (308)—but apparently just to while away the time. He so misses the social meaning of his story that he tells it while they take a breather from subduing another slave revolt, the architect's. That obliviousness confirms how completely he has failed to take the humane inspiration he claims from the boy-symbol. Instead, in Yoknapatawpha as in Haiti, he sides with those who had rejected him.

The architect's plight is little different from the Haitians', though he is less likely to take his slavery for granted, which can make it seem worse. Still, he is just one isolated slave. For Sutpen and the others, black and white, who track the architect down, chasing him is entertaining, like hunting for fox or bear. In one sense that makes it worse, the sense that made Faulkner write many times about the horror of hunting for people and the dignity of the hunted. But in another sense the story of one hunted man, enslaved for two years and isolated enough to make the hunt for him mere sport, seems trivial next to the generations of abuse behind the secret rites and mutilated bodies, the voodoo, smoke, and drums of a mass revolt in Haiti.

Haiti looms in the background of *Absalom, Absalom!* as an exaggeration of the Mississippi South and an embodiment of American slaveholders' fears of revolt, justice, and revenge. The memory of Haitian rebellion portends an upsurging through voodoo of the independent black culture that slavery suppressed and that the Jim Crow system continued to suppress on into the time Faulkner wrote *Absalom, Absalom!* In effect, in its tale-within-a-tale structure, the novel wraps the scenes of Haiti in a series of three envelopes. Surrounding the story of Haiti, and represented by it, is the milder story of Sutpen's cruelty to the architect. Surrounding Sutpen's cruelty to the architect—who designs the plantation house—is the whole system of slavery and plantations. Surrounding the rather easy condemnation of slavery and plantations, for someone writing in the second third of the twentieth century, is the social control and daily degradation of segregation that Faulkner was raised to take for granted and was just beginning to see critically.

All this has little to do with the historical Haiti, where slavery came to a bloody end by 1803, five years before Sutpen is even born. Led by Toussaint-Louverture, Haiti's slaves revolted and established an independent nation. It is hard to know how to take Faulkner's blatant anachronism. It could be mere oversight, though Toussaint and the Haitian revolution are too well known to make that likely. It could be Faulkner's reminder of how little we can trust a tale that passes through so many narrators. Shreve himself, later in the book, mocks the story's melodrama by calling the scene of revolt "Porto Rico or Haiti or wherever" (372, 373). We can even note that Sutpen finds the architect in Martinique (39), another French Caribbean colony where slavery and the sugar crop were still going strong in the 1830s and there were major slave uprisings in 1815, 1822, and 1848. (The revolt in *Absalom,* apparently more or less confined to one plantation, takes place a year or two before Sutpen appears in Mississippi in 1833.) Faulkner underlines the lack of concern for Haitian history when Quentin refers in frank ignorance to the "barns or granaries or whatever it is you harvest sugar into" (310). This is not Haiti then so much as a projection of American anxieties, indicating a guilty fear that white

Americans have done things horrible enough to provoke so frightfully violent and—to most Americans—incomprehensibly foreign a revenge. And it also indicates an opposite fantasy that whites have done nothing horrible enough to provoke a response they cannot still put down with one bold strong white man, as when "something had to be done so he [Sutpen] put the musket down and went out and subdued them" (316–17).

Next to the Haitian slave revolt, chasing the architect seems like a game. But it is still astonishing that Grandfather and the other men of Jefferson come along to watch, without a murmur of objection. Their passivity makes them share the blame for Sutpen's abusiveness, no less so when at last they catch the architect and Grandfather idealizes his courage, dignity, and ingenuity in the chase (321). The kindness in Grandfather's appreciation feels incongruous after he calmly goes along with Sutpen's manhunt, for the fun. Quentin himself relays the story without a murmur, and in the process dredges up again the old legend of Sutpen's "wild niggers," seemingly with no critical distance on its lurid bigotry. Like his father, his main source for the story, Quentin sometimes seems too taken up with the supposed romance of the past to question it. That shows Quentin's closeness to the culture that he fears Sutpen's story might represent, and his closeness makes Quentin's questioning, when he does question, more agonized and strenuous.

Sutpen too has cause to question. Years later, as his design collapses with the return of Bon, he wonders where he made what he thinks of with inert simplicity as his "mistake" (329, 334). To him, morality is a calculation in "arithmetic" (365) and conscience a legal formula, as if the "ingredients of morality were like the ingredients of pie or cake and once you had measured them and balanced them and mixed them and put them into the oven it was all finished and nothing but pie or cake could come out" (328). Thus despite all his troubles, even as his family and home and the economic and political system they depend on crumble around him, it never occurs to Sutpen to question principles or people. He thinks only to use them. Someone interested in making something new or different would question, but the only new thing Sutpen wants is a role for himself in the old things he is determined to repeat.

Sutpen's breathtakingly literal and self-destructive compulsion to repeat his past evokes a poverty of imagination as deep as his childhood poverty of dollars and learning. Just as he cannot imagine any more elaborate challenge to his teacher's words about the West Indies than to ask if the teacher was really reading from the book, so he cannot build his resentment of the plantation owner into anything more than the dullest repetition. And so, to authenticate the power over his slaves that others would see as founded in legal principle and social custom, he brutally literalizes it by besting his slaves one by one in bloody physical contest. When Sutpen tries to explain himself, he only reveals the more his paucity of imaginative understanding. In a typical instance, he tells General Compson: "I made no attempt to keep not only that which I might consider myself to have earned at the risk of my life but which had been given to me by signed testimonials, but on the contrary I declined and resigned all right and claim to this in order that I might repair whatever injustice I might be considered to have done by so providing for the two persons whom I might be considered to have deprived of anything I might later possess" (330). Passages like this are among the funniest and most appalling in this novel of underrated comedy. That is how Sutpen talks about his *marriage*. It is the Sutpen style that General Compson calls "forensic verbiage" (307). Sutpen can follow the winding trail of parallel syntax ("not only that which ... but which ... , but on the contrary") and strike the notes of high-sounding but empty Latinate rhyme and redundancy ("declined and resigned all right and claim"). Like a lawyer, simply to cover himself he can summon ornate locutions that invoke all probabilities and unlikely possibilities (five uses of the word "might"). But he never comes out and names what is really at stake, never says why he left his wife, how he *felt* about it, and how *she* felt about it.

Part of the irony is that this Sutpen who has so little imagination has all through the novel been the absent object of everyone else's imagination. At last Faulkner brings him on to speak for himself, at however many removes of intermediating narrators, and he has less understanding of Thomas Sutpen than Quentin, Quentin's father, Quentin's grandfather, and now even Quentin's roommate, who all know so much less about him. Sutpen believes that he thinks mostly of the future, thinks about how to build his role as plantation master, and then, as events collapse around him, how to start over and build a new plantation, and then, when events collapse again, to rebuild it, always fixed on what comes next. In a land absorbed with its past, a land shuddering in the aftermath of devastating war, Rosa notes that Sutpen the war hero tells no war stories (200–201). He seems to fear that a glance to the past would distract him from his determination about the future. But Sutpen's vision of the future is never more than a fixed stare at the past he feels driven to re-create, no matter how futile the re-creation starts to look. It seems fitting, then, that he is killed by a man with a scythe, as if by Father Time wielding the traditional instrument and symbol of death.

Time catches up with Thomas Sutpen, and yet Faulkner's use of the scythe feels so heavy-handedly portentous that perhaps it works more satirically than symbolically, becoming less a symbol than a mock symbol, a warning against the resort to simple or ready symbols like Sutpen's boy at the door or Rosa's demon. Shreve, always the quickest to see a chance for satire, introduces the murder weapon as "that scythe, symbolic laurel of a caesar's triumph" (223), garbling scythe, laurel, and triumph, three ancient but otherwise unrelated images, and so ridiculing the overdetermination, the convenience of ready meaning in the scythe. To see Jones as the fateful instrument of time or the carrier of symbolic meaning could blot out the anguish that motivates his revenge—at least in Quentin's story—by making Jones into a concept, a figure from a cardboard allegory, rather than the character of psychological pathos suggested by his response to Sutpen's insult. Faulkner intensifies the poignance in Jones's murder of Sutpen, Milly, and their daughter by rendering it with the high drama of indirection rather than the low drama of bloodlust—so much so that some readers do not even realize what Jones has done (364)—and then by finishing it off with the more obvious but more pathetic drama of Wash's soundless and defiant suicide, which makes his final act of revenge more sadly and grotesquely an act of defeat.

Faulkner treats Wash's last moments with intense psychological sympathy, making Quentin imagine much of the scene by going into what could have been Wash's own thoughts. He never does that for Sutpen. It is one thing to observe Sutpen's compulsion to repeat, or the evasion of feeling in his fixed purpose and oratorical stiffness, but another thing to know or understand the feelings that he evades and that drive on his compulsion. There are, in other words, severe limits to how psychologically we can peer into Sutpen. He is a character rather than a person, and a character much less like a person than some of the novel's other characters, such as Wash Jones in this final scene, or Quentin or Rosa. As a character he sustains a grim two-dimensionality that a person could never carry off except as a facade. All of us may be doomed to repetition, as Freud thought. But the starkness of Sutpen's compulsive repetition has a quality of allegorical exaggeration, suggesting a character possessed by a force larger than the psychological impulse of any character or person, a force too menacing to be close cousin to the more conventional, half-hearted allegory of scythe-swinging Wash Jones as Father Time. Faulkner builds some of that threatful quality by mystery, by never allowing us to face Sutpen or his emotions squarely, and also by setting Sutpen's repetition and the other characters' fascination with it in the wider context of *Absalom, Absalom!*'s struggle with repetition at large.

REPETITION AND CHANGE

If Sutpen is trapped in repetition, is the novel's repetition any less constricting, any less stagnating than Sutpen's? Rosa is described as "Cassandralike" (22, 72). For Cassandra, who could predict the future, even the future is the past and thus confined to repeating what she already foresees. Does not Quentin keep listening to and telling the same story over and over again, first with Rosa, then with his father, then with his father again after he returns from the Sutpen house, and then yet again with Shreve? And this is not the first time with Shreve, since Shreve already knows so much about it. Is Quentin any less constrained by repetition than Sutpen? Quentin acknowledges the fear:

> *Yes. Maybe we are both Father. Maybe nothing ever happens once and is finished. Maybe happen is never once but like ripples maybe on water after the pebble sinks, the ripples moving on, spreading, the pool attached by a narrow umbilical water-cord to the next pool which the first pool feeds, has fed, did feed, let this second pool contain a different temperature of water, a different molecularity of having seen, felt, remembered, reflect in a different tone the infinite unchanging sky, it doesn't matter: that pebble's watery echo whose fall it did not even see moves across its surface too at the original ripple-space, to the old ineradicable rhythm.* (326)

It sounds lovely, but suspect. Rosa, earlier on, thinks the opposite. She describes Sutpen's return: *"He rode up the drive and into our lives again and left no ripple save those instantaneous and incredible tears"* (199). Rosa, who can find neither rhyme, reason, nor shadow of excuse, cannot see the connections between events. Surely she is rash to think that Sutpen leaves no ripple in Judith's emotion simply because Judith stoically holds her emotions inside. If Rosa overlooks connections, perhaps Quentin sees them too readily.

Here Quentin sees the dilemma of repetition, which seems to dissolve his own identity into his father's, and strives to convert it into something less perilous, strives to make it gentle, natural, inevitable. If it is inevitable, then he will bear no responsibility for it. Readers of *The Sound and the Fury*, recalling that Quentin will drown himself, can recognize his romantic attraction to what he self-deceptively supposes will be peaceful watery ultimacies. In the same way, here in *Absalom, Absalom!* Quentin imagines Wash Jones and Sutpen sitting together in an afterlife and serenely contemplating what might have gone wrong while they were alive (234). Readers typically take that scene as a description of Sutpen and Wash Jones, but it tells far more about Quentin, who imagines it. Quentin's vision of a peaceful afterlife, for instance, has no likeness to Judith's equally revealing vision of an afterlife too crushed and crowded for peace (158–59). If, as Quentin thinks in his reverie, nothing is ever "once," if nothing can have its own distinctness, then "different" things are not truly different, and it all "doesn't matter," which is a comforting thought to those like Quentin who fear that it matters very much indeed.

In *The Sound and the Fury,* Quentin remembers or imagines his father chiding him for believing that suicide can remove him to a peaceful, afterlife finality, that he can free himself from the burdens of change. But here in *Absalom, Absalom!,* Mr. Compson too feels the strain of repetition. As we have seen, he envies his image of Sutpen and Bon as self-created and parentless, which is to say, free from the burden of repeating the past. Sutpen's image as the founder, the man at the origin, seems part of what makes him so fascinating for Jefferson legend, including for Rosa (13), though when Mr. Compson tells about Sutpen the founder, in chapters 2 and 3, he ignores his later story about the Sutpen whose founding is all mimicry. Just as Mr. Compson imagines the Bon he envies as a man without parents—"a young man of worldly elegance and assurance beyond his years, handsome, apparently wealthy and with for background the shadowy figure of a legal guardian rather than any parents" (89–90)—so he also imagines that Bon's son looks "as if he had no childhood, . . . as if he had not been human born but instead created without agency of man or agony of woman" (245). He thus entertains matching illusions about Sutpen, his son Charles Bon, and his grandson Charles E. St.-V. Bon *before* he knows that the two Charles Bons are son and grandson to Sutpen. In a sense, then, Mr. Compson's image of parentless figures represents his image not only of these particular characters but also of the past itself as "different . . . , simpler and . . . uncomplex" (109–10). To Mr. Compson, the present, doomed to repetition, can never be so simple and free as the originating past.

In a drearier version of the same feeling, Quentin insists that he cannot escape repeating the past, repeating even his own father: *"Am I going to have to hear it all again* he thought *I am going to have to hear it all over again I am already hearing it all over again I am listening to it all over again I shall have to never listen to anything else but this again forever so apparently not only a man never outlives his father but not even his friends and acquaintances do"* (345–46). Quentin does not have to hear it all over again unless he wants to. His insistence seems motivated by the wish—an unconscious wish, allowing him to complain that he doesn't want it that way—to release himself from responsibility for his present, a present only obliquely addressed in *Absalom, Absalom!* but one that grows crushingly dismal in *The Sound and the Fury.*

Repetition of the father becomes an obsession in *Absalom, Absalom!* In the Compsons it covertly takes two opposite forms: the wish to free oneself from repeating the father and the contrary wish to free oneself from responsibility and blame by taking cover in that repetition. Whereas in Thomas Sutpen it overtly takes two other opposite forms: the patriarchal wish to replicate himself with sons, and the denial of the self he does replicate in his son Charles Bon. The Compson plot, already visible in *The Sound and the Fury,* and the Sutpen plot, visible only in *Absalom, Absalom!,* converge when the Compsons tell, repeating from father to son, the story of the Sutpens' incest anxiety.

In *The Sound and the Fury,* Quentin is haunted by incestuous feelings about his sister Caddy. In *Absalom, Absalom!,* chapter 7 becomes a story of brother-sister incest fear, as Henry kills Bon to prevent Bon and their sister Judith from committing incest. (The plural *their* can come as a shock, after so many pages assuming otherwise, and the verbal shock underlines the narrative shock.) Henry's motive for murdering Bon includes the wish to prevent Bon from acting out Henry's own fantasy of incest, especially if we consider Mr. Compson's embroidering of the story, since even before he learned that Bon was Henry and Judith's half-brother, he focused on the special feeling between Henry and Judith, as if to taunt Quentin about Caddy (96–

97, 119, 122–23, 129). That makes Quentin a repetition of Henry. In another sense, it also makes Henry's fear a repetition of Quentin's fear in *The Sound and the Fury,* since that novel was written earlier. Henry's reluctance to murder Bon, indicated by his waiting four years until the last critical moment, makes Henry an anxious figure whom the uneasy Quentin can identify with. And that identification, in turn, makes Quentin ache as he contemplates the limit to their repetition, because Henry's eventual capacity to do the murderous deed mocks Quentin's ludicrous failure in *The Sound and the Fury,* where he sets out to shoot Caddy's lover Dalton Ames and then faints with fright and weakness.

Quentin's repetition of and identification with Henry project him, imaginatively, into the stream of Sutpen's wish to replicate himself with sons. But when Quentin tells the story of Sutpen's effort to get himself a son by Wash Jones's granddaughter Milly, he shapes it through his own preoccupation with incest anxiety, now livened by the discovery that Judith's fiancé was her half-brother. From that perspective, the other side of Rosa's oedipally motivated attraction to Sutpen is Sutpen's attraction—such as it is—first for Rosa, the sister-in-law younger than his daughter, and then for Rosa's replacement, Milly.

Basing his story on what he has heard from his father, Quentin begins by telling about Sutpen and Jones drinking together, placing them as generational peers and in some ways comrades, which reenforces Sutpen's grandfatherly relation to the 15-year-old granddaughter. Then Quentin imagines that Sutpen uses Wash almost as a pander to his own granddaughter. He envisions Sutpen asking Wash to deliver the ribbons and beads that Quentin guesses Sutpen used to ingratiate himself with the girl. Or if Wash did not deliver them, Quentin goes on to guess, still Wash and eventually "all the other men" (353) would know that Sutpen gave her the ribbons, because they would recognize them as coming from the store that Wash ran with Sutpen. That suggests that Quentin enjoys the idea of Wash anticipating and thinking about Sutpen's motives, for surely if the ribbons—which are only Compson speculations anyway—are for sale in the store then anyone else could have bought them. Quentin's and his father's prurient angle shows less subtly when Quentin remarks that the "girl matured fast like girls of that kind do" (352), as if lower-class girls "mature" more quickly, though class divisions can foster such fantasies. Quentin lingers over the sorry spectacle of Judith fitting and sewing a dress for Sutpen to give Milly (355–56), making Sutpen's daughter pander for him to a minor barely half her age, though in that case Quentin claims fact rather than speculation. Either way, he and his father select which incidents to imagine and repeat, and the incidents they choose show the unsettling, unconscious side of Sutpen's attraction to Milly that holds special interest for Mr. Compson and his son.

The conscious side, of course, is hardly more reassuring. Sutpen cares nothing for Milly, except to flaunt his disregard by insulting her. He cares only to produce a son, and through the scene of Sutpen's and Wash's deaths it becomes apparent that *Absalom, Absalom!* depends on Sutpen's obsession with his own patriarchy. With Bon dead and Henry vanished, he still has Clytie and Judith, yet they cannot fulfill his longing. He wants a son. Through the ugly cruelty of Sutpen's obsession, *Absalom, Absalom!*, written by a man who had three brothers and longed for a sister, who had two daughters and no sons, sets itself against patriarchal tradition, against the belief that the production of sons and the passing of property to sons—and perhaps even the passing of stories to sons—must measure the worth of self and family.

The scene's structure dramatizes Sutpen's refusal of feminine worth by dispensing early with his death, which we might expect Faulkner to save for last, and ending instead with the more abstract matter of Sutpen's attitude toward having a daughter. Indeed, Shreve and Quentin long ago hinted that Wash would kill Sutpen with the scythe (223, 228). In any case, the episode actually begins when Quentin mentions that Sutpen didn't come home and that a boy sent to look for him found a body "lying in the weeds" (356). In Faulkner's usual manner, the flamboyant indirectness, the refusal to say outright that Sutpen has been killed, only makes his death more noticeable. Here, also in Faulkner's usual manner, he gives the effect before the cause.

Earlier, he has mentioned that the newborn child is a girl (74, and perhaps 167), but so obscurely that readers, especially first-time readers, are unlikely to remember or even understand the reference. Then, after dispensing early with Sutpen's death, Faulkner and Quentin, in their rearranged sequence, even decline to end with the three unexpected deaths—the granddaughter's, great-granddaughter's, and Wash's—that raise the ante of surprise. Instead, the chapter comes to a halt as Quentin, in effect, explains all the deaths by saying "It was a girl" (365), which makes the baby's gender the story's goal and point.

To set that up, he first moves toward it and then skips past it, saving it for last:

> The old nigger said . . . that he jerked the riding whip toward the pallet and said "Well? Damn your black hide: horse or mare?" and that she told him and that he stood there for a minute and he didn't move at all . . . , and she said she saw his eyes and then his teeth inside his beard and that she would have run then only she couldn't . . . : and then he looked at the girl on the pallet again and said "Well, Milly; too bad you're not a mare too. Then I could give you a decent stall in the stable" and turned and went out. (356–57)

Sutpen asks, in his coarse way, the question that the episode is shaped to answer, and Faulkner leaps past the answer to his reaction, again putting effect before cause. The skipped over answer may seem obvious, but Faulkner veils it by quickly making Shreve miss the point (357). That nudges many readers into going along with Shreve. Moreover, Shreve's error, not just missing the implication that it's a girl but actually taking for granted that it's a boy, comes close to repeating the patriarchal assumptions in Sutpen's obsession, so that when Faulkner draws readers—some of them, at least—into Shreve's mistake, he points a finger of accusation at their complicity in the patriarchal ideology that Sutpen's obsession shows as cruel. And so when Faulkner begins the episode where we might expect him to end it, at Sutpen's death, he gives his readers a feint, a false lead. He makes us think we know where the story is headed, so that he can make it more surprising when he goes beyond Sutpen's death to Wash severing the neckbones of his granddaughter and great-granddaughter, and then takes yet another step to Wash's suicide, and then yet one more to the long-delayed explanation that Sutpen's callousness comes not only because he cares nothing for Milly but also because the child she has born is a girl. And there he stops, with all the emphasis of a sudden halt.

Sutpen's words to Milly repeat the tone of his offense to Rosa when he proposed to her *"as you might say it to a dog"* and then insulted her *"as if he were consulting with Jones or with some other man about a bitch dog or a cow or mare"* (209, 210). At the last, it seems that one more thing Sutpen repeats is the undoing of his own ambitions at every step. For ironically, he seems all along to have had what he wants, right from the Haitian offspring of his first marriage, which repeats itself in three generations of boys (Charles Bon, Ch. E. St.-V. Bon, Jim Bond). But for some reason that we do not know, he rejects his first marriage. When he finds another chance with Ellen, the marriage yields Henry, but Sutpen goes on to sacrifice Henry by delegating him to fend off the Haitian line with a crime that makes him run away. Trying again with Rosa, Sutpen once more ruins his chance. And with Milly he succumbs to his own discouragement when, instead of simply trying again, as would-be patriarchs have done since time immemorial, he gives up on Milly and speaks the words that provoke Wash to kill him.

The capacity to look critically at Sutpen's obsessive repeating and even at Quentin's contorting of Sutpen's story into his own obsessive repeating makes the novel's overarching repetition fundamentally different from the repetition of its individual characters. Sutpen, Mr. Compson, and Quentin are all stuck in self-destructive repetitions, though that shows more sharply for the Compsons when we also read *The Sound and the Fury*. The novel repeats perhaps no less compulsively and no less patriarchally than its characters do. But it builds into its repeating the difference of critical reflection, which cannot purify it but which still distinguishes it from the Sutpens' and even from the Compsons' repeating.

• • •

Indeed, in this second half of *Absalom, Absalom!,* as the Sutpens and Compsons burrow ever deeper into their repetitions, the novel at large takes up some striking changes. We have already reviewed those at the beginning of this chapter, including the leap from hot September in Mississippi to cold January in Massachusetts; the break in narrative sequence—skipping past the ride out to the Sutpen house while still leaving the impression that it somehow makes a difference; Rosa's off-stage death; and a new major character, Shreve.

Shreve changes things dramatically. After Rosa's circuitous abstractness in the italicized chapter 5, Shreve's bluntness makes fun of how everybody else takes the story so seriously. "This old gal, . . . this old dame, this Aunt Rosa," he keeps saying (221), despite Quentin's insistence that Rosa is not his aunt. Shreve senses that the last thing Quentin wants to admit is that he feels drawn into the story like one of the family, and so he mockingly protests Quentin's denial: " 'You mean she was no kin to you, no kin to you at all, that there was actually one Southern Bayard or Guinevere who was no kin to you? then what did she die for?' and that not Shreve's first time, nobody's first time in Cambridge since September: *Tell about the South. What's it like there. What do they do there. Why do they live there. Why do they live at all"* (218).

Shreve's point is not so much that Quentin is responsible for what happens to Rosa, even for her death, as that Quentin *feels* responsible, feels guilty, and that Southerners—satirically represented by stock Southern, pretentiously aristocratic names—feel weighted down self-consciously with the burdens of the past and a sense of difference. Indeed Quentin feels Harvard's questioning so intensely that people in Cambridge seem not only to lump all Southerners together but even to wonder why Southerners would live at all. Some readers, unprepared for the way Faulkner shifts through italics into a mind's interior, assume that people actually ask Quentin why Southerners live at all, but once we recognize those words as Quentin's irritated exaggeration of snobby Harvard curiosity, then the question reflects not only on Northern manners but also on Quentin's readiness to doubt his own self-worth. This is the Quentin who, finding no reason to live at all, will finish his first year at Harvard by committing suicide. And like many a college roommate, Shreve picks up on Quentin's sensibilities, probing and jabbing with a roommate's mixture of mercilessness and kind concern.

Shreve's terms for Rosa—this old gal, this old dame, the "little dream-woman" (226)—mock Rosa's hauteur as well as Quentin's jittery susceptibilities. He highlights the ridiculous in her already half-satirical demonizing by exaggerating it: "this Faustus, this demon, this Beelzebub" (223). Or, sometimes in the same breath, he translates her ornate evasions into something forthright. Rosa goes on and on, as we have seen, insisting how she could tell Quentin about Sutpen's insult and how three words are three too many and three thousand words or sentences that many too few (208), but she never comes out and says what it was, at least not in any of her words that Faulkner includes. Shreve, by contrast, never dodges the point, saying frankly that Sutpen "could approach her in this unbidden April's compounded demonry and suggest that they breed together for test and sample and if it was a boy they would marry" (222).

If Shreve knows what Sutpen said, then unless he simply guesses, Mr. Compson–style, Quentin must tell him, so that sooner or later Rosa must have spoken the words she dreads. But Shreve also remarks that Rosa "couldn't even tell it [the insult] because of who her successor was" (222), which can imply that she never told Quentin after all. Quentin seems to have no knowledge of it after he talks to Rosa, because he refers to Sutpen as having thrown Rosa over (70) when, in Shreve's explanation, Rosa threw Sutpen over. Thus Shreve's explanation may simply repeat what Quentin, after talking to Rosa, hears from Mr. Compson who, it much later turns out, seems to know (348), though we never learn how. He may have guessed, as is his habit. Quentin, at least, refers later to Shreve's version of the insult with no hint of uncertainty (355).

Part of the joke, whether it occurred to Faulkner or not, is that once we finally learn Sutpen's insult, it makes no sense. As long as Sutpen waits to learn the baby's gender before sleeping with another woman, then he cannot increase his chances of begetting a son by switching from one woman to another. If Rosa bears him a daughter, she still has the same chance as any other fertile woman of going on to bear him a son, and more chance than an infertile woman. Maybe the mistake is Faulkner's, or Sutpen's, or even Mr. Compson's, if we're to think of him as the source of Shreve's explanation. It would fit Rosa's words just as well, and sound much more plausible, if Mr. Compson—or whoever else—guessed that Sutpen proposed they wait to see if Rosa were fertile, instead of waiting to see if she bears a son. Still, folk thought on these matters won't always hold to logic. Indeed, even the novel's critics have taken Shreve's explanation at face value. And there isn't much reason to think Faulkner would necessarily work out such little mysteries, especially in a novel that is already about the way we construct contradictory versions of the same events.

Even as such minor riddles multiply, Shreve, as the outsider, relieves the pressure of riddling, ambiguous double-talk, cutting through the rhetoric to explain what other characters mystify. Shreve takes things from earlier in the story and exaggerates them to poke fun at everyone else's credulousness. Sutpen's four wagons of crystal chandeliers and fine furniture (51) Shreve recasts as "six wagons . . . with the crystal tapestries and the Wedgwood chairs" (223). (Wedgwood, as a kind of china, makes no more apt an adjective for chairs than crystal does for tapestry.) He lengthens Rosa's strange engagement, during which her betrothed completely ignores her, from two months to three (212, 226). Where General Compson is befuddled at Sutpen's failure to *explain* how he got to Haiti or ended up in a besieged house during a slave revolt (311) or, after the revolt, got engaged to the plantation owner's daughter, Shreve exaggerates the oddity by recasting Sutpen's silence as forgetfulness: "he didn't remember how he got to Haiti, and then he didn't remember how he got into the house with the niggers surrounding it. Now are you going to tell me he didn't even remember getting married?" (318).

As Shreve repeats the story (221–27), he reviews what we already know, but elides and condenses it to his satirical taste and outsider's skepticism. When Quentin then says that *"he sounds just like Father"* (227, 264), Quentin is wrong. Shreve's storytelling is brash and irreverent, versus Mr. Compson's cynicism and patient luxuriance. To be sure, Quentin's complaint has a kernel of truth, not about Shreve so much as about Quentin. Quentin attracts and feeds on other people's talking to him. The other people vary, but Quentin remains the lesser or dependent party. Thus, if we think of *The Sound and the Fury,* he remains forever bound to his role as the brother who depends on his sister, even though she, in the usual fashion, outgrows her dependence on him.

In Shreve, however, Quentin finds a peer and in that sense someone different from his father. Shreve goads Quentin, telling him, sometimes helpfully, where to take the story (325, 331), but Quentin resists Shreve's impulse to take over: "Wait. . . . Wait, I tell you! . . . I am telling" (345). It becomes something of a roommate's contest. " 'No,' Shreve said; 'You wait. Let me play a while now' " (349). Shreve's verb, *play,* might seem to threaten Quentin's lugubrious seriousness, but it remains a roommate's contest of peers. Their competition takes the novel somewhere it had not been before as Quentin sat and listened or sometimes didn't listen while his betters droned on. By this point, *Absalom, Absalom!* seems, aside from its difficulty, a perfect novel for the college classroom, as it evokes that heady verbal bravery of late nights among new friends come together from widespread places to pursue the common goal—intellectual, social, and personal—of asking questions and telling stories.

QUESTIONS ABOUT PLOT, REVISITED

If we return, once more, to our questions about plot, we no longer need to ask why Sutpen went to New Orleans; the answer is clear. And Shreve has explained why Rosa didn't marry Sutpen. No one seems to doubt his explanation, even if it doesn't entirely make sense. After that, all the answers to our other questions have changed, and again, we have one major new question: 1) why does Henry vanish? 2) why does Henry kill Charles Bon? 3) what is the "something" living in the Sutpen house? and 4) why does Sutpen "repudiate" his first wife?

As we saw at the beginning of this chapter, now that we know Bon is Sutpen's son, we have all the same outward actions as before, but an entirely new set of motives. The bigamy plot drops away to be replaced by a far more threatening plot of incest, giving new answers to the first and second questions. We do not learn that until late in chapter 7, but Quentin and perhaps Shreve learn it long before chapter 6 begins, letting it shape their story even while, on a first reading, we don't know about it.

How Quentin learns about the incest plot is something of a mystery; we could even add it to our list as another question. Quentin says he found out that night when he and Rosa went to see what was living in the Sutpen house, which indicates that the answer to Rosa's question about what was at the Sutpens' might also be the source of Quentin's knowledge. For that reason, the question about how Quentin found out seems more or less the same as the question about what was out there at the Sutpen house.

Which leaves one more question: why does Sutpen "repudiate" his first wife? Many readers like to start guessing. For those who start to "play," as Shreve puts it, who pick up the conjecturing impulse from Mr. Compson, Quentin, and Shreve, it might be hard not to start guessing. But it might also be wise to keep in mind that just because Faulkner provokes us to guess does not mean he will necessarily ever give a certain answer, or even an uncertain one, especially in a novel that puts into question whether we can ever unearth the final facts of the past, the rhymes reasons and shadows of excuse, and whether—if we can unearth them—we can ever truly understand them or must instead, like Mr. Compson and Quentin and Shreve, forever conjecture.

At the same time, that is not to presuppose that we never will find out. It is only to refrain from presupposing either way. Because if we expect answers, we might bias ourselves to find them, to, in effect, imagine them where they are not. And if we expect that answers are impossible, then we might bias ourselves into so much skepticism that we do not see them where they turn up. In *Absalom, Absalom!* we thus find ourselves conjecturing not only about the plot of events, but also about the plot of conjecture itself.

7

Compounded Each of Both
Yet Either Neither:
Chapters 8–9

MISCEGENATION, IRONY, HYSTERIA

To finish reading *Absalom, Absalom!* can turn the process of thinking about it upside down. Getting to the end of any novel, of course, changes the ways we think about it, but for *Absalom* the changes are more extreme and intricate. In that sense it is like a detective novel, where new information helps sort the clues from the false leads, but *Absalom* also ends with more questioning and less certainty than we might expect from a detective novel.

In the final two chapters, the novel's prism of incident and structure shifts yet again, so that the questions we have followed shine in yet another light. Why, the novel asks again, does Henry kill Charles Bon? And this time it answers that Henry kills Charles not to prevent incest between Charles and Judith, but rather, after learning from their father that Bon's mother was part black, he kills Charles to prevent miscegenation.

How does Quentin learn that? Critics have argued a good deal over that question and proposed a variety of answers, which we will soon review, but for now let us say that Quentin, in one of the novel's great surprises and one that answers yet another ongoing question, learns about Bon's mother when he discovers that the "something" living at the Sutpen house is, astonishingly, Henry Sutpen himself, alive and back home after all those years. It seems that Henry—though this is a debatable contention, which we will need to examine more closely—tells Quentin not only that Bon was Sutpen's son but also that Bon's mother was part black. And that information, in turn, answers the question about why Sutpen repudiated his first wife. Which leaves these last two chapters with two radical turning points: one when we learn that Bon's mother was part black (443), and another when we learn that Rosa and Quentin found Henry at the Sutpen house (464).

The new information sharpens much that seemed out of focus before. Why, we need to ask again, did Henry vanish that Christmas Eve in 1860? Part of the surprise is that now, despite the new information, it seems that he vanished for exactly the same reason we were left to suppose in chapter 7. That is, he vanished in protest when Sutpen told him that Bon was Sutpen's son and Henry and Judith's half-brother. According to the new version in chapter 8, not until that somber evening when Henry sees his father in an army tent in 1864 does his father tell him about Bon's mother, which provokes Henry to murder.

The new information also explains Sutpen's cryptic language to General Compson when he stops by the general's office several years after the Christmas Eve revelation to Henry in 1860 but before the second revelation to Henry in 1864. General Compson repeats Sutpen's words to his son, who repeats them to his son, who repeats them to Shreve, but the Compsons cannot quite understand the words until after Quentin learns about Bon's father and mother. Perhaps it is too much to expect that none of them would figure it out. Indeed, many readers start guessing, and a few crack the code of Sutpen's speech right away, without needing to wait another quarter of the novel until we hear about Sutpen's later words to Henry in the tent. With hindsight, at least, Sutpen's obscure references all fall into place. He explains to General Compson that he has already discarded his first marriage. "Yet," he continues,

> I am now faced with a second necessity to choose, the curious factor of which is . . . that either choice which I might make, either course which I might choose, leads to the same result: either I destroy my design with my own hand, which will happen if I am forced to play my last trump card, or do nothing, let matters take the course which I know they will take and see my design complete itself quite normally and naturally and successfully to the public eye, yet to my own in such fashion as to be a mockery and a betrayal of that little boy who approached that door fifty years ago and was turned away . . . , this second choice devolving out of that first one which in its turn was forced on me as the result of an agreement, an arrangement which I had entered in good faith, concealing nothing, while the other party or parties to it concealed from me the one very factor which would destroy the entire plan and design. (341–42)

Since he has already told Henry that Bon is his son, and that failed to turn Henry against Bon, then Sutpen's "trump," so far held in reserve, must be the card he later plays by telling Henry that Bon is part black. If he doesn't tell that to Henry, then Judith and Bon will marry, destroying his design not in the public eye but in his own. But if he does tell Henry, then Henry—he seems to anticipate—will murder Bon, which will also destroy the design, apparently because Henry, Sutpen's heir, will suffer in punishment or shame or, more likely, will run away.

With hindsight, perhaps too much hindsight, these seem pretty clearly to be Sutpen's thoughts, though to follow them through in detail can take us over the border into writing our own novel and leave us wondering about such details as how Sutpen anticipates that it might take something as extreme as murder to prevent the marriage. And we might think Henry would have little to fear, in Mississippi in 1865, if he can claim that he killed to prevent incest and miscegenation. On the other hand, to claim such a defense would require him to own up publicly to Judith's willingness to marry Bon, not exactly something a Mississippi plantation heir in 1865 would like to scatter to the public.

Which raises another issue less extravagantly speculative. All Sutpen's tortuous, legalistic reasoning assumes that the burden of decision falls entirely on himself and on Henry and Bon: on the men. No consideration of Judith's feelings ever enters his maze of ill-applied logic. Perhaps, as Mr. Compson speculates (97, 336), no one ever tells her what her father objects to in Bon. Or perhaps, as Shreve speculates, they tell her and she doesn't care (412, 426). We never know. Here among these characters who have no critical distance on the patriarchal focus of their obsession, and in this book that has at least some critical distance on its own and its characters' patriarchal focus, the responsibility of decision goes all to men. As a father and son and the son's roommate all strain to analyze the Sutpens' motives, the woman in question enters their thoughts only as the object of male exchange.

Once we fit all these patriarchal pieces together the result leaves a trail of retrospective irony over dozens of moments earlier in the novel, as before when we suddenly learned that Bon was Sutpen's son. But the ironic light shines only on a rereading, except as first-time readers remember and think back over earlier passages. For example, Rosa's remark that Sutpen "created two children" who go on "to destroy one another and his own line" (18), which we studied to begin our reading of the novel, refers to Henry and Judith. Then after we learn that Bon is Sutpen's child, her words ironically apply to Henry and Bon. And now those same words inadvertently predict the deaths of Henry and Clytie. In chapter 9 we learn that Clytie sets the house ablaze (at least Shreve supposes she does, though no one sees her do it or hears her tell Jim Bond to do it), burning herself and her half-brother Henry to death.

More narrowly in the realm of irony and even, by now, comic irony, the new information casts a different light on Mr. Compson's story of Bon and bigamy, right from the opening words of his tale: "Mr. Compson raised his feet once more to the railing, the letter in his hand and the hand looking almost as dark as a negro's against his linen leg. 'Because Henry loved Bon. He repudiated blood birthright and material security for his sake, for the sake of this man who was at least an intending bigamist even if not an out and out blackguard' " (110). Here the ironies multiply. Although Mr. Compson's tale does not depend on the race of Bon's concubine-wife, because it makes bigamy the issue and not race, it is nevertheless so laden with undertones of racial superiority and so far from anticipating that Henry objects not to Bon's earlier marriage but rather to his black ancestors, that the blackness of Mr. Compson's own hand mocks his comfortable assumption, as he rests his feet on the railing, that he sits above the fray. Bon, it turns out, is a "blackguard" indeed, though not in the sense Mr. Compson means. And "blackguard" is already a loaded word for readers of *The Sound and the Fury,* where Caddy Compson engages herself to a nitwit scoundrel to cover her pregnancy, leaving the horrified Quentin to think and plead over and over, "Not that blackguard Caddy." Like so many things that Mr. Compson says, his remark here seems primed to rile Quentin over Quentin's inability to let go of Caddy emotionally, and over the identification that his clinging leads to—in *Absalom, Absalom!*—with Henry's murder of Judith's fiancé.

Mr. Compson's tale of bigamy culminates when he imagines that Bon, after meandering from one reason to another, finally clinches his defense of the New Orleans marriage by playing one last rhetorical card, "the trump now, the voice gentle now: 'Have you forgot that this woman, this child, are niggers? You, Henry Sutpen of Sutpen's Hundred in Mississippi? You, talking of marriage, a wedding, here?' " (146). Again the ironies multiply. Bon's "trump," as Mr. Compson imagines it, is exactly what their father will turn on Bon by telling Henry about Bon's mother, even using the same word, "trump." Mr. Compson, as he makes up the story of Bon's trump, has already heard of Sutpen's trump from General Compson but doesn't yet know enough to understand it. And that only begins the complications, for readers do not learn the story of Sutpen's trump that here gives Mr. Compson his language until several chapters and two hundred pages later (341), which is still another chapter and a hundred pages before we learn the information that allows us to understand it, the information that Bon's mother was part black (443). That, in turn, allows us to look back and see that Mr. Compson's Bon unknowingly dismisses his marriage and its offspring for exactly the reason his father gives for dismissing Bon and his mother.

Thus when Bon claims it makes no sense for Henry Sutpen of Sutpen's Hundred to talk of Bon's arrangement as a true marriage, he cannot know how ironically appropriate is his lingering over Henry's identity as a Sutpen. If Sutpen had not thought in the same way that Mr. Compson's Bon now thinks and that Mr. Compson's Henry objects to, then there would never have been any Henry. Sutpen would never have left Bon's mother and gone to Mississippi to marry again. In tossing off his sidedoor marriage because his wife is a "nigger," Mr. Compson's Bon, to defend himself against Henry, therefore repeats his father's heartless verdict against Bon himself, and that, yet more ironically, is the same cruel judgment that we will later learn Henry repeats when he decides to kill Bon.

Moreover, just as Mr. Compson's Bon, speaking to Henry, makes light of his marriage, so also Shreve's Bon, in yet another wry turn of the ironic screw, coolly dismisses the same more or less marriage while speaking to his mother:

> "Why not? All young men do it. The ceremony too. I didn't set out to get the child, but now that I have. . . . [*sic*] It's not a bad child, either" and she watching him, glaring at him and not being able to say what she would because she had put off too long now saying what she could: "But you. This is different" and he . . . : "Why not? Men seem to have to marry some day, sooner or later. And this is one whom I know, who makes me no trouble. And with the ceremony, that bother, already done. And as for a little matter like a spot of negro blood—" (384–85)

Shreve makes up everything he says about Bon's mother without even giving her a name, though Faulkner calls her Eulalia Bon in the Genealogy at the end. In this scene, Shreve's Eulalia (to use the name for convenience) resents that Bon does to his wife exactly what, unbeknownst to him, his father did to her, and so she glares at him without explanation. She refuses to tell what his father did, and so in her outrage she starts to sputter out sentences that she dares not finish: "But you." The irony stings when he shrugs off the issue in trivializing terms: a "little matter" and a "spot of negro blood." At this point, first-time readers still do not know, though a few guess, that Eulalia herself has a "spot of negro blood" and that Sutpen has repudiated her for exactly that reason. But Shreve knows, and since Shreve makes up this whole incident, his knowledge begets the irony.

From another perspective, it might seem that, rather than doing to his wife what his father did to his mother, Bon does the opposite: he defends the marriage, whereas his father callously cast his mother aside. From that perspective, Shreve's Eulalia, crestfallen at her son's marriage to a woman who is part black, would seem to have bought into the ideology that she is a victim of. Nevertheless she senses—it scarcely takes much insight—the placid casualness of her son's attachment to a woman who is no plantation heiress like herself, but a slave bought at market, which leaves their relation hardly reciprocal. He never says he marries for love, but only because, well, "Why not?"— and because she makes him no trouble. But sooner or later everyone makes trouble, or has trouble projected onto them. Bon's mother, as Shreve imagines her, sees the shallowness and transience of her son's commitment.

Even a moment already so complex as when Quentin imagines the words between Judith and Charles Etienne Saint-Valery Bon, after Etienne returns from his travels and his own marriage to a Negro, now becomes vastly more complicated in light of the information that Sutpen's first wife was part black. That makes Etienne Bon's marriage at least the third in a line between men who at least seem white and women who, even when no darker, seem or, like Eulalia, come to seem black. And so when Quentin imagines Judith pleading to Etienne that he discard his wife, the scene now resonates with our ignorance about whether Judith ever knew that Etienne's father and grandfather, Judith's father, did the same or almost the same thing. Quentin imagines her saying to Etienne, *"And as for the child, all right. Didn't my own father beget one? and he none the worse for it?"* (260). These words set off an entirely new set of associations with the hindsight of rereading. On a first reading, Judith seems to refer to Clytie. On a second reading, she still refers to Clytie but could also refer to Etienne's own father, though the number she uses ("one") and the emphasis that he was none the worse for it make that inescapable possibility harder to sustain. Still, we must remember that Judith never says any of these words any more than Eulalia says the other words to Bon or Bon says the words to Eulalia. Quentin, like Shreve in the other scene, makes the words up, and Quentin knows about Bon's father and mother just as Shreve does.

All these dialogues, therefore, tell more about Quentin, Shreve, and Faulkner than about Judith or Eulalia. In this patriarchally obsessed novel, we learn little about the women characters, often not even their names, such as the names of Sutpen's first wife (until the Genealogy), or her more or less daughter-in-law, the so-called octoroon, or *her* daughter-in-law, the so-called apelike charcoal companion. About Eulalia especially we know nothing beyond the barest outline: her wealthy Haitian background, short-lived marriage, and relocation to New Orleans. But we learn much about what the men think or imagine about the women, and that tells something about what those men consider worth thinking about, and what Faulkner supposes matters most to men and perhaps to people in general.

To make so much pivot on the melodramatically delayed discovery that Bon is part black is wildly to sensationalize the ordinary. The whites of Faulkner's world treat miscegenation with a kind of hysteria, which the novel responds to with horrified fascination. The mere possibility of miscegenation wipes out all other considerations. Even so grievous an issue as incest drops aside once Sutpen sounds the alarm about miscegenation. *"You are my brother,"* says Henry to Bon in the last version of any dialogue between them. *"No I'm not,"* answers Bon. *"I'm the nigger that's going to sleep with your sister"* (446). Whether or not Bon believes in such terms, his words dare Henry to confirm them. If Henry will murder Bon to prevent the miscegenation even after accepting the incest, then Bon can tell Henry, *"So it's the miscegenation, not the incest, which you cant bear"* (445).

But is Bon truly "black"? He is, as American culture has usually defined those terms and concepts. For in America, unlike in most other New World slave cultures, to have any black ancestry is to be black. The system, designed to create and sustain a class of property for a class of property owners, cannot be reciprocal: to have any white ancestry is not to be white. In the word *octoroon,* companion to words like *mulatto* (of the same root as "mule") and *quadroon, Absalom, Absalom!* admits a trace of the obsessively classifying language that reached American English from other slave cultures in the Caribbean and South and Central America, and the novel continues that obsession in its characters' impulse to insist that people fit into a category. But unlike the cultures that give us such words, in American culture there have generally been only two categories: black and white, those who could be slaves and those who could own slaves. That is, to Thomas and Henry Sutpen, and to Quentin and Shreve, by the end of *Absalom, Absalom!* Bon is simply black, "the black son of a bitch" (448), in Shreve's words. (Perhaps Shreve chooses his crude words out of satire, mocking the whole system of classification and everyone's confidence in it, as he so often turns satirical on other subjects, but here I see no satirical context.) In Bon's fate and the fate of his son, Faulkner exposes the tragedy in the human urge to insist on categorizing each other, on thinking that everyone is either one of us or one of them, and that no one can fit in between categories or defy categories altogether.

All this is deeply embedded in American culture and to some extent in more than just American culture. Much earlier in the novel, in another of those moments that the new information about Bon's parentage gives a retrospective coating of irony, Mr. Compson tries to explain that even after Sutpen became the "biggest single landowner and cotton-planter in the county" some people always suspected something sinister in his past. "There were," he says, "some among his fellow citizens who believed even yet that there was a nigger in the woodpile somewhere" (86, 87). The expression "a nigger in the woodpile," which refers crassly to a suspicious or evil secret hidden in the past, connects also to racist jokes about whites giving birth to dark babies who thereby reveal the whites' forgotten or secret black ancestors. Kate Chopin's famous story "Désirée's Baby" trades on such tales. In that context Mr. Compson's typically casual remark carries much more meaning than he intends. It gives shape to a stock racist fear among some whites that somewhere deep in their past they are not truly white, a fear that vents the social resentment they feel toward black competition, and also vents a private, psychological doubt of their own authenticity in other matters than race. American whites have often chosen racial resentment as the medium or even the dumping ground for doubts about class and self, leading the culture at large to develop a deep hysteria over miscegenation—over something that in itself, apart from the hysteria over it, might scarcely be remarkable enough to need a separate word.

Faulkner was born in the region and time that institutionalized that hysteria into an elaborate, so-called Jim Crow system of segregation.[1] Even before he was ready to criticize that reaction through direct address to social or political institutions, as he later did cautiously in the 1950s, Faulkner began to expose its tragedy and tindery explosiveness in his fiction, first in "Dry September" (1931) and then much more ambitiously in *Light in August* (1932; see also "Elly," 1934, a much less well known story). By the time he reached *Absalom, Absalom!* he was familiar enough with the subject to approach it ironically as well as tragically. It does indeed look silly that so much in the novel changes simply because Bon turns out to have a black great-great-great (or something like that) grandparent. The silliness, the pointlessness, finally makes the meaning that people attribute to it all the more tragic.

THE EPISTEMOLOGY OF PERSPECTIVELESS EXPLANATION; OR, HOW DOES QUENTIN FIND OUT?

So much then rides on Quentin's discovery that Bon is part black, but Quentin never comes right out and announces his discovery or explains exactly how he discovers it, leaving critics to argue over how he finds out or indeed whether he knows at all. Because of the way *Absalom, Absalom!* questions the grounds and possibility of knowledge itself, many critics believe that its manner of asserting or obscuring Quentin's knowledge can provide a test for the novel's epistemology, its concept of whether and how we can know.

These matters have been hotly debated, and I will try to group and summarize the various arguments and then sift through them and pursue my own development of those that seem to make most sense. I will also claim that the alternatives among the more credible interpretations do not really lead to opposing views of the novel's epistemology, which remains radical whether or not we believe that Quentin ever really finds out about Bon's black ancestry.

The various approaches can be gathered into three or four groups. Many critics claim, or simply assume, that Quentin never finds out and only conjectures or intuits that Bon was part black. That makes it less certain, or at least a different kind of knowledge. The alternative is that someone tells Quentin. Some critics believe, as I am inclined to, that Henry tells him when Quentin sees Henry upstairs in the Sutpen house, and a third group of critics believes that someone else tells him (several candidates have been named). Perhaps a fourth approach is possible, as I will suggest, by supposing that Quentin learns partly from Henry and partly by conjecture.

Many critics refer to conjecture and intuition as if they were interchangeable, but conjecture describes a reasonable surmise from actual yet insufficient evidence, whereas intuition refers to something quite different, to interior knowledge reached independently of evidence. In this case, there is plenty of evidence. As we have seen, Sutpen's elaborate but cryptic talk to General Compson about the "trump" he might play and how his first wife concealed from him the "one very factor which would destroy" (342) his design allows a few readers to guess that Sutpen's Haitian wife, Bon's mother, was part black, so that Quentin has enough clues for conjecture and too many for intuition. Moreover, critics who dismiss the notion that Bon is part black because they see it as intuition—whether they call it that or not—overlook the evidence that gives it, if not certainty, then still the grounding of credible conjecture. They offer no alternative reading of Sutpen's talk about his trump card and how he tossed aside his marriage because of what he calls a "fact which had been foisted upon me without my knowledge . . . , which meant the absolute and irrevocable negation of the design" (341).

Certainly *Absalom* primes us to see conjecture, since most of the novel depends on it. Chapter 8, where we learn about Bon's black ancestry, is rife with conjecture. Shreve, to name the most spectacular example, makes up the intense and elaborate story of Eulalia Bon and her lawyer. But the breadth and audacity of conjecture does not mean that everything is conjectured. Readers of this complicated novel some-times grasp after something they can be certain of, even if they can be certain of no more than uncertainty itself. Thus many critics, mesmer-ized by the brazen conjecturing, treat everything as conjectured. Many others, mesmerized by the evocatively conjectured details, treat conjec-tured and reported matter as if there were no issue of conjecture at all, as if it were all alike and all certain (in the limited sense that a fiction can be certain). Until recent years, most criticism of *Absalom, Absalom!* fell prey to one or the other of those two opposite oversights, either of which flattens the novel's vast complexity.

Shreve, for example, does not invent Eulalia Bon and her lawyer from scratch, as is often claimed. For we know that Bon's father cold-bloodedly discarded Bon's mother, that he nevertheless left her most of her fortune, and that her son—and so she too (taking us barely into conjecture)—moved to New Orleans. Mr. Compson, as well, has referred to Bon's "legal guardian" (90). Shreve makes up the personalities, obsessions, and conversations that form the bulk of his story, but not everything. It does not follow that because Shreve makes up or conjectures so much, therefore anything of obscure origins must be conjectured. Of course, those who claim that Quentin and Shreve conjecture Bon's ancestry are in the awkward position of trying to prove a negative. For unless the novel directly asserts that Quentin and

Shreve reach their conclusion by conjecture, the only way to argue that they do is to contest the claims that they reach it by some other means.

Those who argue for conjecture do submit one passage that they think directly asserts that Quentin and Shreve rely on conjecture to determine Bon's ancestry. According to Shreve, Clytie "didn't tell" Quentin

> in so many words because she was still keeping that secret . . . ; she didn't tell you, it just came out of the terror and the fear . . . : and she looked at you and you saw it was not rage but terror, and not nigger terror because it was not about herself but was about whatever it was that was up stairs, that she had kept hidden up there for almost four years; and she didn't tell you in the actual words because even in the terror she kept the secret; nevertheless she told you, or at least all of a sudden you knew— (437–38)

Shreve never says that Quentin determines Bon's ancestry by conjecture. Nor is it clear that Shreve isn't conjecturing himself, after his fashion, something about Quentin. All that this passage proves is that Shreve conjectures that Quentin conjectured that Henry was upstairs even before Quentin went on to see that for himself. It can seem to mean more, because at this point we do not yet know that Henry was upstairs, so that when Shreve says "you knew—" he seems to refer to whatever crucial thing Quentin is about to learn, especially because Shreve's sentence never gets to its object (*what* Quentin knew), which gives it a portentous sound that tempts us to fill in the most momentous possibilities. But it turns out that on this evening Quentin discovers, even if partly by conjecture, three different crucial things: that Henry is alive and at home, that Bon was Sutpen's son, and that Bon's mother was part black. Shreve, however, refers only to "whatever it was that was up stairs, that she had kept hidden." It makes more sense to say that a person is upstairs than that the details of a person's heritage are upstairs, so that I read Shreve as guessing that Quentin guessed Henry was there, and not, more complicatedly, that he was there, and that his best friend and enemy was his half-brother, and that his half-brother's mother was part black.

Some readers conclude from the same passage that Clytie herself tells Quentin about Bon. That idea seems to arise from the desperate eagerness for explanation into which so complicated a novel propels us, for part of the point is that Clytie does *not* tell anything to Quentin. Nevertheless, other candidates besides Clytie have been nominated for the role of Quentin's informer. Some readers seize upon Quentin's remark that "Grandfather didn't tell" Mr. Compson "all of it" (332), which out of context can make it sound as if Grandfather knew about Bon's parentage and therefore could have told Quentin. But the novel never mentions any dialogue between Quentin and his grandfather, who, according to the Appendix to *The Sound and the Fury,* died in 1900 when Quentin would be about 10. There is no motive for Grandfather to conceal anything, nor does the novel ever pursue that idea. The larger context makes it unmistakable that the things General Compson did not tell his son were simply the things he did not know. Quentin, for example, soon refers twice to "Grandfather not knowing" (339, 340). Shreve checks to make sure: "Your old man," he begins. "When your grandfather was telling this to him, he didn't know any more what your grandfather was talking about than your grandfather knew what the demon was talking about when the demon told it to him, did he? And when your old man told it to you, you wouldn't have known what anybody was talking about if you hadn't been out there and seen Clytie. Is that right?" (342). Quentin agrees, which pretty well demolishes the idea that he learned from his grandfather, but resuscitates the idea that he learned from Clytie.

That, in turn, vexes adherents of the notion that Quentin gets his information from Henry. They sometimes claim, though, that at that point Shreve does not yet know that Quentin met Henry and knows only that Quentin got his information at the Sutpen house. But there's no evidence for that. They seem on firmer ground in arguing that we seem to have a full account of the little dialogue between Clytie and Quentin, with no unaccounted for time for them to speak more than Faulkner renders (437–38, 460–61, 462).

The only other candidate for Quentin's informer, besides Henry, is Rosa. But Faulkner, resorting to his usual tricks, skips most of Quentin and Rosa's ride back to Jefferson (462–63). His playful habit of leaping over things is, after all, what obscures the matter in the first place, leaving us to figure out and to wonder whether we should even try to figure out how Quentin gets his information. But what little description Faulkner provides makes Rosa seem too much in shock to talk. Nor is there any sign that Henry tells her anything about Bon. The mere presence of Henry would be enough to set off her stupor, though Henry would more readily tell her about Bon than tell Quentin. Some critics point to her surly jibe at Jim Bond, "You aint any Sutpen!" (462), as evidence that she still doesn't know that Charles Bon, Bond's grandfather, was Sutpen's son. But if she doesn't know, then what would provoke her to deny a connection that otherwise sounds so farfetched? Her sneer seems, on the contrary, to indicate that she has just discovered that Bond is Sutpen's great-grandson and that she lashes out in a futile effort to pretend it isn't so. In any case, if Rosa tells Quentin about Bon's parentage, then she herself would have learned it from Henry, since she doesn't know before she sees him, and that would be almost as if Henry tells Quentin directly.

Neither Faulkner, in his own or the novel's exterior narrative voice, nor any character ever says outright that Henry tells Quentin, but many critics, including this one, believe that Faulkner definitely though not clearly implies that Henry tells Quentin. If Henry does tell, there still remains a question about how much he tells. Those who emphasize Henry as a source tend to see him as revealing that Bon was Sutpen's son and was part black, but there are more modest alternatives. He could tell about the incest and not about the miscegenation, or he could tell about both without specifying that his father told him about the incest on that Christmas Eve in 1860 and then, playing his trump card under the army tent in 1864, about the miscegenation. In either of those cases, Henry would leave Quentin, perhaps with the help of his always ready father or the no less eager Shreve, to fill in the more glaring gaps, which do not seem difficult to fill in, given what Sutpen told General Compson.

Doubters of the Henry thesis have raised several additional objections. Apparently Faulkner was slow to make up his mind, and different stages in the manuscript have Quentin coming at his information in different ways. Early drafts variously have Judith knowing all about Bon and have Judith herself tell Mr. Compson long ago, or have Rosa knowing that Bon was Sutpen's son, or let Sutpen make it clear to General Compson that he told Henry on Christmas Eve that Bon was Henry's brother. Even a late manuscript fragment has Quentin and Shreve distinguishing explicitly between Henry's knowledge about the incest and his knowledge about the miscegenation. In the full-length manuscript, Faulkner wrote and then canceled passages that have Sutpen telling General Compson that Bon was his son and was part black.[2] The point, however, is not that these manuscripts offer some buried clue to what really happens in the novel. On the contrary, they show the alternatives that Faulkner explicitly decided against.

Other skeptics, claiming that Mr. Compson knew about Bon's parentage all along, having heard from his father who heard from Sutpen, point to an early passage that first-time readers often race by but that sometimes strikes rereaders with astonishment. Mr. Compson says that Sutpen "named Clytie as he named them all, the one before Clytie and Henry and Judith even" (73). This can come as a shock, on a rereading, if we recall that we do not learn Bon was Sutpen's son until late in the book. That can lead us to forget that even apart from this early reference and slightly before we learn that Bon was Sutpen's son (331), we already hear and even have it reiterated that Sutpen had a son by his marriage in Haiti (327, 329). Thus General Compson has long known about the son in Haiti, though readers do not learn about it until Quentin recounts Sutpen's past in chapter 7. But Sutpen never told General Compson that the son in Haiti was Charles Bon. The general's story about Haiti therefore does nothing to help Mr. Compson explain the story of Bon and Henry.

Indeed, the idea that Mr. Compson has known all along about Bon flies in the face of a vast array of material that assumes otherwise. As we have seen, Quentin tells Shreve that his father did not know

(332, 342). Mr. Compson's whole story about how the fear of bigamy drives Henry to kill Bon would be impossible if he knew that Bon was Henry's brother, because incest would be so much more threatening than bigamy, and much of Mr. Compson's story depends in great detail on his not knowing that Bon was Sutpen's son (e.g., 114–16, 119, 130). Nor would he refer to Etienne Bon as a "sixteenth-part black" (244) if he knew that Etienne was part black on his father's side as well as on his octoroon mother's side.

All this argues against the alternatives to Henry as Quentin's source, but offers no evidence in favor of Henry. Such evidence as there is, though I find it convincing, is indirect, in Faulkner's typical manner, which leaves knowledge itself a tenuous concept, clung to in any given instance, if at all, only by an equally tenuous cobbling together of materials themselves tenuously grasped after.

Faulkner has fun with his uncertainties as well as or in the process of using them to reach after profundities. Before Quentin discovers Henry upstairs at the Sutpen house, Faulkner, in another of those moments that later acquire a retrospective irony, has Quentin, as he walks to the rotting old house with Rosa, "thinking, wishing that Henry were there to stop Miss Coldfield and turn them back" (454). Then, still before he talks to Henry and learns about Bon, he sees Jim Bond and, supposing him the only person living there who has any future, thinks of him as the "scion, the heir, the apparent (though not obvious)" (461), little knowing, at that point, how literally but unobviously he is indeed the scion and heir, or at least the sad mockery of one. When at last Quentin goes to see what Rosa has seen upstairs, still before we know that she has seen Henry, Faulkner unabashedly extends his already radical postponing of explanation. For the scene, not revealed until chapter 9, takes place, as we have said, between the time present of chapters 1–5 and the time present of chapters 6–9, and right from the beginning of chapter 6 it is clear that much of the book's second half depends on this scene at the Sutpen house even while we do not know what happened there. When we finally approach the long-postponed and sure-to-be climactic moment, Faulkner throws out another jolt of delay. As Rosa comes downstairs in a daze from what-ever she has seen, Quentin "stood there thinking, 'I should go with her' and then, 'But I must see too now. I will have to. Maybe I shall be sorry tomorrow, but I must see.' So when he came back down the stairs . . ." (462).

Then at last Faulkner gives not the scene of Quentin's confronta-tion with Henry, but instead a twice-removed version of it, as Quentin remembers how later that night he remembered confronting Henry (464–65). Even that doesn't tell much, only that Henry is there, and has been for four years, and is dying, but nothing about Bon. Many readers have been led astray by Quentin's feverish, multilayered re-membering. They point to the bare-bones dialogue and rashly conclude that Henry said nothing about Bon. But the point is not to present a full transcript of Quentin's dialogue with Henry. On the contrary, Faulkner renders this scene in a form and tone that have little in common with the earlier scene between Quentin and Clytie, which gives the impression of a complete transcript. Here, with his usual flair for flamboyant indirectness, Faulkner obscures the scene he has set us up to anticipate. That enhances the surprise in finding Henry by ra-tioning that surprise so radically that the scarcity raises its value in the closed market of interpretive economy. Meanwhile, the same scarcity also shifts our attention from the surprise itself to Quentin's reaction to it, as Faulkner's elaborate delays and hints, on this matter as on so many others, dramatize that the facts themselves matter less than our attitudes to them, in the same way that Bon's parentage would make no difference apart from the culture's and the characters' attitudes to incest and miscegenation.

The evidence that Henry tells Quentin about Bon rests mostly on Quentin's explanation to Shreve that he learned the crucial facts when he went out to the Sutpen house. Since he seems not to have learned his information from anyone else, and Henry has a chance to share the information, and only Henry clearly even has the information to share, that leaves only Henry as Quentin's source. The obstacle to figuring all that out is that when Quentin explains it, in chapter 7, the novel has revealed that Bon was Sutpen's son but not yet that Bon was part black, which makes it impossible to recognize the full role of Quentin's explanation without bringing to bear a good deal of hindsight.

Nevertheless, the hindsight pays off. For if we return to the two crucial moments when Shreve interrupts Quentin, the first time to ask how his father could know about what Quentin was telling when it so contradicts Mr. Compson's story about the bigamy threat (332), and the second time, having heard Quentin's explanation, to repeat it back to him (342), they now appear in a considerably brighter light than when we examined them before as explanations of how Quentin found out that Bon was Sutpen's son. When Shreve interrupts Quentin, we have just learned that Bon is Sutpen's son (331), and so we focus on that. We do not yet know that Bon is also part black, and so we cannot follow any references to it. But Quentin knows, and Shreve apparently has learned from Quentin. For in the first instance it seems and in the second it is unmistakable that Shreve interrupts not when Quentin refers to Bon as Sutpen's son, but when Quentin refers to the problem Sutpen saw in Bon's being part black, even though—and here lies the source of confusion—we cannot tell that that is what Quentin refers to until we look back through the lens of hindsight.

In the second and plainer instance, Quentin reports what Sutpen said the day that Sutpen pondered whether to play his trump card, which has nothing to do with Bon being his son and everything to do with Bon being part black. Sutpen describes his decision to desert his first wife as "forced on me as the result of an agreement, an arrangement which I had entered in good faith, concealing nothing, while the other party or parties to it concealed from me the one very factor which would destroy the entire plan and design which I had been working toward, concealed it so well that it was not until after the child was born that I discovered that this factor existed—" (342). Shreve interrupts at exactly that point to confirm that none of this was intelligible until Quentin went out to the Sutpen house and found more information. Until we ourselves get that information, we cannot clearly follow these words, but will probably assimilate them vaguely to our new knowledge that Sutpen was Bon's father. Once we learn also that Bon's mother, Sutpen's first wife, was part black, then that is clearly what these words are about, and therefore it is clearly what Quentin agrees he learned on the night he went to the Sutpen house. If his knowledge were conjecture, it would not need to be reached on that particular night. He could have reached it then, but there would be no reason to make such a point of it. The only reason to make a point about Quentin acquiring his knowledge on that particular night is to connect his discovery to something special about that night, and the special event of that night is his discovery of Henry.

On those grounds it seems that Faulkner clearly, even if with extravagant circuitousness, indicates that Quentin learns about both Bon's father and Bon's mother from Henry, who learned from his own father. It is odd, someone might object, that Faulkner waits so long to tell about or have Quentin refer directly to Bon's black ancestry, though certainly Faulkner suffered no fear of oddity. In any case, he and his character Quentin already wait pretty long to tell that Bon was Sutpen's son, and Quentin first mentions that notion not on his own initiative but only when Shreve brings it up, so we have the oddity regardless of how Quentin learns about Bon's mother.

At the same time, other evidence supports the view that Quentin learns from Henry. Another moment in the narrative refers, though again circuitously, to what Henry tells Quentin, and it comes significantly right after we learn that Sutpen supposedly told Henry, that evening in the army tent, that Bon's mother was part black:

> He must not marry her, Henry. His mother's father told me that her mother had been a Spanish woman. I believed him; it was not until after he was born that I found out that his mother was part negro.
> Nor did Henry ever say that he did not remember leaving the tent. He remembers all of it. (443)

Faulkner has a brilliance for concocting ways to come so close and yet stay so far. This strange passage, by referring to what Henry did not say, implies by inversion that he did say something. Whom he said it to is hardly any clearer, but Quentin seems to be the implied listener. The sudden shift to present tense takes us past Henry's 1864 confrontation with his father and suggests his encounter with Quentin in 1909, roughly the same time as the Massachusetts present of 1910. The narrative soon skips a line and returns temporarily to the past tense (444), as if to set this section apart both for Sutpen's revelation to Henry, which doubles as Faulkner's revelation to his readers, and for this one oblique candidate for a reference to Henry's memory in 1909. Syntactically indirect as it is by itself, in context the reference turns yet more indirect, because not until the next chapter do we find out that Quentin ever meets Henry, and without that knowledge we cannot attribute much significance to what Henry said, let alone to the claim that his saying anything at all is implied by the assertion that he did not say something else.[3]

Part of the difficulty here comes from the extraordinarily unusual status of narrative perspective in this scene. It is hard to tell whose words these are, or whether to attribute them to any character or characters at all. Faulkner undermines the very idea of individual perspective, the same sort of individual perspective that he leads us to pay so much attention to through the rest of the novel, where it matters a great deal that Mr. Compson says one thing and Rosa or Shreve says another. For a long stretch, Shreve has been doing the talking, but not in the usual way of this novel or other novels or of speech outside novels. Even before he starts to talk, the distinctiveness of his identity dissolves away "in the cold room where there was now not two of them but four, the two who breathed not individuals now yet something both more and less than twins" (367). Faulkner, or his external narrator, insists many times that "it was Shreve speaking, though . . . it might have been either of them and was in a sense both" (378). He does not deny the differences between Shreve and Quentin. They disagree, for example, over what kind of story it would take to describe Bon's love for Judith (395–417), and Shreve taunts Quentin over his sexual inexperience and touchiness about love for sisters (404). Rather than deny their differences, Faulkner says more modestly that "it did not matter to either of them which one did the talking" (395, 417) because "each before the demand, the requirement, forgave condoned and forgot the faulting of the other" (395).

To say that it did not matter to them is not the same, as some commentators assume, as saying that it did not matter. In one instance, Shreve and Quentin think how Henry would later remember seeing Judith and Bon through the window as they stroll about the garden at a lover's pace amid blooms of "jasmine, spiraea, honeysuckle, perhaps . . . Cherokee roses," while unbeknownst to them Sutpen announces to Henry that Bon is Sutpen's son and therefore must not marry Judith. The external narrator, however, goes on to remark that those are "blooms which Shreve possibly had never heard [of] and never seen . . . and it would not matter here that the time had been winter in that garden too and hence no bloom nor leaf even if there had been someone to walk there and be seen there since, judged by subsequent events, it had been night in the garden also. But that did not matter because it had been so long ago. It did not matter to them (Quentin and Shreve) anyway" (368). Faulkner never actually adds that it might matter to us, but his otherwise needless word "anyway" and his specification of Quentin and Shreve suggest as much. How serious is the excuse that "it had been so long ago"? It sounds like a comically irrelevant dodge or a profound comment on how the passing of time filters abstract truths from the cloud of inconsequent trivialities. But if we are asked to disavow the befuddled calculating over minutia that this book so often teasingly provokes, then it looks strange that the narrator "judges by subsequent events" only to use the judgment to argue that judgments like that do not matter. It seems that to Faulkner or his narrator they do matter, or at least cannot be escaped.

Only such judgment allows Faulkner to distinguish what Quentin and Shreve say from what might meet a more exacting or at least a different standard. Not a standard of truth, for in this novel's evanescent atmosphere that seems too transcendently credulous. But Faulkner still distinguishes what Quentin and Shreve say from what might meet some criteria of plausibility or potential corroboration. He refers to the "two of them creating between them, out of the rag-tag and bob-ends of old tales and talking, people who perhaps had never existed at all anywhere, who, shadows, were shadows not of flesh and blood which had lived and died but shadows in turn of what were . . . shades too" (379). This places no less value on the shadows they create, but it differentiates them from historical personages. Or more radically, it undermines the notion that historical personages can be understood in some stable way, without being shaped by our understanding. When we look to the past, we cannot simply observe. Inevitably, we look in selected ways and at selected things, following conscious and uncon-scious social and personal criteria that also lead us not to look at other things or in other ways, so that history becomes a novelistic fiction rather than an objective realm of fact and truth.

The shadows that Shreve and Quentin create are therefore false, but not false to them, and their feelings matter, since in many—though not all—respects the novel here is about Quentin and Shreve rather than about Henry and Bon. Quentin and Shreve's tale contains "fault-ings both in the creating of this shade whom they discussed (rather, existed in) and in the hearing and sifting and discarding the false and conserving what seemed true, or fit the preconceived—in order to overpass to love, where there might be paradox and inconsistency but nothing fault nor false" (395). Here Faulkner does not, as many readers have assumed, reject the notion of falseness. He only says that *in love* there *might* be nothing false, which makes for two considerable qualifications. As Quentin and Shreve shape their account to fit their preconceptions, including their feelings about love, it becomes a story in the self-preoccupied romantic tradition of individual ardor and adventure far more than, for example, such other possibilities as an economic story of the abuses of class privilege or the collapse of a nascent agrarian feudalism under the onslaught of exterior industrial hegemony, or an anthropological tale of attitudes towards incest and family relations, or a ribald comedy of mistaken identities and long-lost relatives. All those alternatives, like Shreve and Quentin's, might bring their own mix of falseness to other standards and of truth—or at least lack of falseness—to their own standards, as Shreve acknowledges and even insists by his almost rapturous repeating of the word "maybe" (e.g., five times on 370).

What then of falsity or plausibility—if truth is not an available alternative—for the Henry who hears from Sutpen, in that special land of italics, that Bon's mother was *"part negro"*? Some readers think that the pleasure Faulkner takes in shadows of shades and his radically skeptical fondness for paradox and inconsistency oblige us to toss into the air the whole idea of asking what "really" happened to Henry, or what his father "really" told him, or what Bon's parentage "really" was. Certainly the story that all these uncertain comments set up, the frenzied tale of Eulalia Bon and her extortion-crazy lawyer, runs outside the circle of what's plausible. But it does not follow, as some readers assume, that the same applies to the tale of Sutpen, Henry, and Bon that grows out of Shreve's tale about Eulalia and the lawyer. It does not follow, because something happens in between, something difficult to identify but vaguely signaled by the shift to italics.

Across the many pages of Shreve's story that lead up to the italics, Faulkner scatters the narrative with skeptical qualifiers but balances his skepticism with words of approval. He remarks, for example, that Shreve and Quentin at least "believed" (e.g., 418, 419, 420) what Shreve says and that, in a remarkable expression, it is "probably true enough" (419, twice). But all such commentary disappears in the italicized story of Henry's pivotal confrontation with his father in the army tent and his following confrontation with Bon as he thinks about what their father told him. The transition to italics comes amid what may be the most audacious moment of narrative conjuring in a novel already given to breaking the customary bounds of narrative possibility. Shreve has been talking, and then, says Faulkner,

he ceased again. It was just as well, since he had no listener. Perhaps he was aware of it. Then suddenly he had no talker either, though possibly he was not aware of this. Because now neither of them was there. They were both in Carolina and the time was forty-six years ago, and it was not even four now but compounded still further, since now both of them were Henry Sutpen and both of them were Bon, compounded each of both yet either neither, smelling the very smoke which had blown and faded away forty-six years ago from the *bivouac fires burning in a pine grove, the gaunt and ragged men sitting or lying about.* (438–39)

Faulkner vaults over the wall of readerly expectation and hangs in the air, levitating outside the ontology of ordinary life and ordinary storytelling. The strangeness all comes before the italics begin, so that the italics do not themselves make for the change, but only give this unidentified flying narrative one more stamp of confirmation. The actual flip into italics comes at a point where there is otherwise no seam in the storytelling or even the syntax, just as later, when the italics disappear, Shreve immediately takes up the same story they tell, as if he himself had been speaking the italicized words (447). Other than that, nothing indicates that Shreve speaks or even thinks those words, so that the italics seem to represent not his speech but instead something analogous to though not the same as his speech or to a set of thoughts that he and Quentin share. In that sense they work much like the italics of Rosa's unspeakable monologue in chapter 5, except that here in chapter 8 the less bounded, mistier move into and then out of italics makes the transition to strangeness more noticeable.

Here then, in the voice that reveals the information or conjecture that crucially separates Bon and his mother as *"part negro,"* Quentin and Shreve deny that separation and become Bon—and become Henry too. Identities merge, and voice itself disappears. When Faulkner says that Shreve had no listener, that is clear enough; we have already been told that Quentin was not listening to Mr. Compson or Rosa (159–60, 215–16, and later on 466). But what does it mean to be told not, as we might expect, that Shreve is no longer a talker, but rather that suddenly he *has* no talker? Apparently, he resigns voice and submits to some alternative—we might call it vision if there were any ocular metaphors, but here Faulkner leaves us with no such conveniently anthropomorphic handles. Whatever it is that usurps voice, it no longer proceeds from within the subjective self, as voice can seem to. Sprung free of the self, it heralds the possibility of escaping the limits of Shreve and Quentin's romantic preconceptions, their preoccupation with what they imagine as personal or individual.

If Shreve, then, is no longer "there," who is the "he" who "possibly" is aware that he has no talker? Possibilities that once excluded each other now merge paradoxically until the voice no longer a voice, the perspective that we are left to rely on in the most pivotal scene in the novel, the scene that wedges Henry's discoveries about Bon into Quentin's discovery 46 years later about Henry is "compounded each of both yet either neither." This is the scene that Henry takes as incitement to kill Bon. Not this scene in itself, which would be falsely simple in the land of either neither, but this scene as filtered through the other scene that mediates and no doubt distorts it, the skipped over and long-suspended scene of Quentin's discovery that falls out of the narrative between chapters 5 and 6. At the end, at last, it falls back in, but only in either neither fashion, first at the incomprehensible remove of these italics, and then at the two removes of Quentin's memory of remembering it later that night. As Faulkner grasps after all impossible complementary and contradictory alternatives at once, trying, as he later often said in interviews, to put it all in one sentence, the result is to dramatize the irrecoverability of direct experience and the hopeless measures we strain after in compensation, trying to recover what must stay forever lost.

The italics thus give special access to what we can never quite reach. That special quality of unreal knowledge seems finally more real, in the sense that, if it would be too transcendental to call it truthful, then at least its spiral of compoundings makes it differently or more intensely "there." It does not become more "realistic," since the narrative has floated outside and above any literal or even literary realism. Rather, it becomes in a sense hyperreal, more present, more urgently "there" than anything in all the reasonable and cautious hedging of Shreve's maybes and probablies and probably true enoughs.

Still, it is hard to tell where it comes from. It owes something to Henry, as backhandedly attributed when the italics acknowledge, as we have seen, that *"nor did Henry ever say."* And it owes something to Quentin and Shreve, who transmit and embellish whatever might come from Henry. Aside from that, it misses the point to try to identify the nature or authority or voice for this passage in any ordinary way, to say, for example, as some people have, that it is Shreve or Quentin's hallucination or dream or vision. It is something like all those things, but it is also pointedly different from anything we have a name for, so that to apply a term to it is to miss the point of its insisted-on extravagance.

The leap into another realm comes unbroken by attribution to Shreve or Quentin. Readers who try to resist the strangeness and iron Faulkner down into something more familiar typically take these italicized scenes as the characters' conjecture. But in pointed contrast to all the earlier conjectures, where each time Faulkner identifies the characters as conjecturing, this time he says that "neither of them was there." The many critics who without much thinking about it or with only a little wriggling try to attribute this passage in some even relatively ordinary sense to Quentin or Shreve miss how far it goes beyond the methods of ordinary realism. Ordinarily, any passage comes *either* from the perspective of a character *or* from the perspective of the exterior narrator or author. But the point of this passage is to present some other kind of voice, a sourceless voice that cannot be traced to a definable perspective, and thus to break the bounds of ordinary narrative that is always either *or* neither and replace it with something actually either *and* neither at once, without even a conjunction (or, and) between them. And so in one limited sense I propose a conservative reading of the novel's radical epistemology by suggesting that we do get an outline of facts that the story pivots on. But in another sense, I propose a radical reading, ontologically, by suggesting that we get that outline revealed from a fictional perspective or even perspectivelessness that the narrative places outside our ordinary sense of the possibilities of being. Here more than anywhere else Faulkner anticipates the metafictional, postmodernist effort by many later writers to cast aside ordinary conventions of realism and shape alternative fictional worlds, playfully parodying the idea that fiction must or even can reproduce a world outside of fiction.

And so I would claim that we do indeed know that Bon was Sutpen's son and part black and that we know those things through the relation of this otherworldly mist of italics to such passages as those where Shreve asks Quentin how he found out and Quentin explains that he learned when he went to the Sutpen house. The point in characterizing that knowledge as derived in part through such otherworldly means is not to be mushily relativist, not to insist that we can never establish even a provisional, fictional truth to explain the Sutpen story—because Faulkner goes to too great a length to clarify, carefully including—even, as we have seen, adding in revision—Quentin's helpful explanations to Shreve's questions. Nor, on the other hand, is the point to clamp the novel down into inflexible certainties, for Faulkner also goes to too great a length to obscure. The point is to provoke a lush Faulknerian sensation of knowledge as all extravagantly and at once an available resource and an inescapable problem, compounded each of both yet either neither.

INCEST, HENRY, AND QUENTIN: TOO MANY BROTHERS

If the whole plot pivots on Henry's response to the fear of miscegenation, then we might ask why Faulkner toys so long with all the worry about incest. How we answer that question will tell a great deal about how we read the novel. But perhaps the question, though almost inevitable, launches from a false premise. It is not Faulkner who writes off incest; it is Henry. It is not Faulkner who can abide incest but cannot abide miscegenation. That, again, is Henry. The burden of Faulkner's story is that Henry is not the indulgently romanticized individual personality of Quentin and Shreve's tale but rather, like the characters who are part black and part white, Henry takes on the role of representing something in the culture around him. To understand what Henry represents, we need to look squarely at what some readers and even some scholarly critics turn away from: incest is a crime, miscegenation assuredly is not.

My experience is that many readers get caught up in the series of supposed crimes that explain the story. Bigamy (in our culture) is a crime, even if one we sometimes find a little amusing. Incest is a crime. Until well after Faulkner wrote *Absalom, Absalom!* many states outlawed interracial marriage, and so miscegenation, which some people still object to or quietly take offense at, must therefore also be a crime—or thus many readers seem to assume, often without reflection. But it is exactly such reflection that Faulkner's story should provoke. And it is the reluctance to take up such reflection that in part draws him into his series and that surely his series is, nevertheless, partly designed to expose, as Faulkner is both the product and the critic of his surroundings. Henry and that stratum of his world that he represents mistake miscegenation for a crime, and in *Absalom, Absalom!* that mistake is itself the crime, and murder its form of expression.

Henry murders his brother in a time of national fratricide. For Henry, the possibility of miscegenation in his family figures on a personal scale and with narrowly sexual immediacy a major part of what the Civil War was fought over on a national scale, namely, the relation between the races. The private arena of murder over race betrays the grungy underside of public pieties about fighting to defend states' rights and Southern nationalism, while the public arena of war betrays how the private acts of Sutpens and their kind are not individual decisions so much as instances in a vaster and more broadly social effort to cling to privilege.

And so when the weight shifts from Henry's fear of incest to his fear of miscegenation, the aftershock may remind us of the earlier shift from his supposed fear of bigamy to his fear of incest, but ideologically they bear little resemblance. Each surprising discovery shifts the emphasis, but in a different way. Once we learn that Bon was Sutpen's son, then it becomes apparent, as even Mr. Compson admits he could not help suspecting, that nobody ever cared about the possibility of bigamy since they would never consider a master's alliance with his slave a bona fide marriage. But once we learn that Bon was part black, which raises the possibility of miscegenation, then the possibility of incest does not go away. Incest replaces bigamy, but miscegenation adds to rather than replacing incest. Or it replaces incest not so much in the circumstances as in Henry's reaction to them.

Assuming, that is, that we trust Shreve's story or at least trust the story in italics that accords with it, as I tried to show in the last section that we can. Thus Faulkner sets up a competition between fear of incest and fear of miscegenation as ways to explain Henry's motives for murdering his brother. Some readers assume that all the uncertainty leaves the two explanations suspended with equal authority, but that underestimates the weight given to Henry's terror of miscegenation when the novel veers into its outlandish world of either neither, including the italicized Bon's claim to Henry that *it's the miscegenation, not the incest, which you cant bear* (445).

Much is therefore at stake when Henry decides to go along with the incest and then, after learning about the miscegenation, objects so intensely that he kills Bon to prevent it. There are good and powerful grounds to oppose incest, but the grounds to oppose miscegenation, however powerful, are noxious and unacceptable. Henry decides, in effect, that Bon is less his brother than, as the italicized Bon puts it, the *nigger that's going to sleep with your sister* (446). Henry's murder of Bon thus doubly denies brotherhood, by killing a brother and by subordinating the brotherly relation to his fear of cross-racial intimacy. Where love conflicts with hate, he chooses hate.

Put another way, in words that Shreve imagines for Bon, Bon has *too many brothers* (385). In the last moment before Sutpen plays his trump with Henry, Henry has become so close to Bon that his very words to their father ape Bon's words to Henry (442–43, 436). The trump must therefore strike hard to make him decide to kill the brother he has grown so close to. The killing of a brother took on intensely personal reverberations for Faulkner as he wrote *Absalom, Absalom!* Faulkner had introduced his youngest brother, Dean, to flying, and in 1935 Dean crashed and died in a plane that Faulkner had sold him. Faulkner was devastated. He spent the days comforting his mother and Dean's pregnant wife, and in the nights he spread his manuscript on their kitchen table and carried his pain into yet more feverish work on it. Perhaps that pain in some way contributed to the novel, but by then the novel was well under way. Faulkner had long before decided that Henry would kill his brother, so that we can never know how his surge of grief and guilty feelings after Dean's death may, for better or worse, have influenced the novel.

At the novel's end, when Quentin finds Henry upstairs in the Sutpen house, it grows clearer than ever how radically Faulkner separates the structure of his tale from the structure of the way he tells it. He takes a single incident that in the tale itself includes three surprises—Quentin's discovery of Henry, Henry's revelation that Bon was Sutpen's son, and Henry's other revelation that Bon was part black—and splits it into three separate incidents of narrative, one revealing the threat of incest, another the threat—or what Henry takes as a threat—of miscegenation, and another more obliquely revealing Henry as the source of those earlier revelations. The effect is to put the ideological onus on Henry. It makes the shape of *Absalom, Absalom!* as a whole reproduce not the pattern of Quentin's experience, in which all three of those discoveries come at once, but rather the pattern of Henry's experience, because, as we have seen, Sutpen's talk about his carefully withheld trump card, coming between his encounter with Henry on Christmas Eve of 1860 and his next encounter with Henry in 1864, reveals that Henry's two discoveries about Bon come at two separate times. By separating the two revelations, Faulkner underscores Henry's choice to let one and not the other tip him over into the decision to murder, and in that way he underscores the culture's choice of hate over love, which Henry comes to represent.

This elaborate pattern of withheld information is only the most extreme example of a technique that Faulkner relies on throughout the novel. He suspends Mr. Compson's letter for over half the book (218–470). He interrupts Wash Jones's summons to Rosa at the end of chapter 3 and picks it up again to finish chapter 4. In the sequence of chapters 1 through 5, as we have seen, he withholds chapter 5 until the end even though it falls chronologically between chapters 1 and 2. He has Shreve tell us things that Shreve must have learned earlier from Quentin, even though Quentin never mentions them in any dialogue that gets into the novel. The point is not necessarily to keep us from knowing or finding out so much as it is to goad our interest and draw us into the *process* of knowledge and discovery, with all that process's implications as we choose one fork or another along the path of decision, such as when we choose whether to look critically at Henry's decision to accept incest and his refusal to accept miscegenation, a refusal so deep that he will murder to enforce it. If we do not accept that challenge to think critically, then, like some readers, we might stop short of realizing that the killing is a murder. It is easy to get drawn into Quentin's identification with Henry and lose critical distance, and some readers still feel reluctant to think critically about the hysterical fear of miscegenation. But the intricate delay of the idea that miscegenation is even at issue can dramatize and call into question that reluctance.

Faulkner even has enough perspective to joke about his reliance on postponed and roundabout explanation, as when he has Quentin say that Sutpen, talking late into the night, "finally did stop and back up and start over again with at least some regard for cause and effect even if none for logical sequence and continuity" (308). But joking aside, Faulkner's own rearrangements of cause and effect, logical sequence and continuity carry a burden of persuasion. His delays finally tell us more than they keep from us.

The end of chapter 1 presents in microcosm this larger process of step-by-step revelation, of dramatizing by delay. There (30–33) Rosa reveals first that Sutpen pitted his slaves against one another like dogs or cocks, then that Ellen saw him do it, and then that she found Sutpen joining in the fights himself. Then she tells that he made Henry watch, and only last does she say that Judith—and Clytie—*chose* to watch. Each new revelation jacks the surprise a little higher, until this one scene almost predicts the rest of the novel. Henry screams, vomits, and cries at the sight of his father facing blacks as physical equals. Judith watches silently and with patient strength, leaving us to guess what she thinks, just as she will leave us to guess her reactions later. Clytie stands by Judith.

The very existence of Clytie, appearing here for the first time and identified only as a Sutpen face on the negro girl beside Judith, leaves it plain that Sutpen has no objections to miscegenation so long as he retains the position of power. To Sutpen, as to many other beneficiaries of the slave system, there is nothing objectionable in coerced sex between a white master and a black slave. The objection that propels the novel's plot is not to miscegenation itself but more specifically to miscegenation between equals, as in Sutpen's first marriage. Henry, so far as we know, makes no complaint about Bon's arrangement with his octoroon slave, but to Henry and his father an actual marriage between the races is another matter, and even worth killing your own brother or, apparently, son to prevent. That would never come across the same way without Faulkner postponing the revelations to isolate one motive from another, to isolate the fear of miscegenation from the much more sympathetic fear of incest, and to use the competition between motives to dramatize that the choice for hate includes the denial of love.

The shaping of narrative according to the sequence of Henry's discoveries rather than Quentin's discoveries leaves us to ask what all this drama about Henry's motives has to do with Quentin. When Quentin discovers Henry at the Sutpen house, the two planes of plot, one from the nineteenth century and one from the twentieth, converge. What had sometimes seemed to Quentin like idle history, as he sat not listening to Rosa, becomes part of his present. When he discovers Henry not only ill but apparently, after being primed by his meeting with Rosa, even ready to talk, Quentin gets pulled in. He becomes a participant in the story he has listened to all his life as if it were mere legend, and he becomes a participant at the Sutpen level. Hence Shreve's insistent joking about Rosa as Quentin's aunt riles Quentin because it treats him as if he were a Sutpen, as if he were another brother to this man who has "too many brothers," who comes to represent, especially for the Quentin of *The Sound and the Fury*, the anguish of brotherhood itself. By killing to protect what he sees as his sister's honor, as Quentin in *The Sound and the Fury* has tried and ludicrously failed to do, Henry denies his brotherhood to one sibling to affirm it—by his twisted standards, at least—to another. Shreve, like Mr. Compson when he tells Quentin that perhaps Rosa considers him "partly responsible through heredity for what happened to her and her family" (11), jabs at exactly what Quentin fears and wants to deny.

Perhaps the most stinging reason Quentin's collision with Henry makes him identify with the Sutpen siblings is that it echoes an earlier scene that has already mesmerized him, the scene of Henry's dubious triumph after the murder that sets the whole novel going. Perhaps that scene fascinates him because, as we have said, Quentin has tried and failed to commit a similar murder in *The Sound and the Fury*, or perhaps, confining ourselves to this one novel, he simply identifies with another tortured and patrician young man. In any case, when Quentin drives out to the Sutpen house he joins Rosa in reenacting the earlier scene from the day when Henry shot Bon and Wash Jones drove Rosa out to see what happened. Rosa expected to find Henry triumphant or at least explanatory, Judith grieving, and Bon dead. Apparently she didn't think to expect anything from Clytie. In imagination, Quentin has taken over for himself the same scene that Rosa rode out to find, shaping it into a stark vignette that he "could not pass." He imagines Henry telling Judith that he has killed Bon, staging the conversation in "brief staccato sentences like slaps," which Faulkner sets apart in italics "with twelve or fourteen words and most of these the same words repeated two or three times so that when you boiled it down they did it with eight or ten" (215–16, 218–19).

But when Rosa arrived at the Sutpen house, she found none of the idealized, romanticized images she had looked forward to, no corpse, no bereavement, no Henry. Instead, she found Clytie trying to stop her from mounting the stairs in a long moment eerily suspended. Now in 1909, Rosa still cherishes the memory of those romantic expectations, but after 44 years she can recognize and ridicule them: *"What did I expect? I, self-mesmered fool, come twelve miles expecting—what? Henry perhaps, to emerge . . . and say 'Why, it's Rosa, Aunt Rosa. Wake up, Aunt Rosa; wake up'?"* (174–75).

At last in chapter 9 we discover that when Rosa rides out again to the Sutpen house, this time with Quentin, she again finds Clytie trying to stop her from mounting the stairs in a long moment eerily suspended. And this time at the top of the stairs she finds exactly what she has chided herself for expecting to find before: Henry. Again Quentin cannot pass a crucial conversation with Henry that, through the transformation of memory, becomes an italicized string of "brief staccato slaps with twelve or fourteen words and most of those the same words repeated." The difference is that this time Quentin participates firsthand, speaking the brief staccato sentences himself.

In *The Sound and the Fury*, Quentin is stuck trying to repeat what, from his late adolescent perspective, seems like the secure pleasure of childhood with Caddy, until he kills himself to keep from growing into adult independence. Now, already prey to a fantasy of repetition in his own life, he enters the Sutpen repetition, until it feels to him as if he has become another of those obsessive Sutpen repeaters. Unable to defend his sister's honor, Quentin becomes a feeble repetition of Henry, who is a feeble repetition of his father Thomas. Each clings to an inflexible design. Quentin dreams of prepubescent bliss between brother and sister in *The Sound and the Fury*. Henry dreams of something much the same with Judith, and for that reason he will allow the incest. To Henry, Judith's incestuous marriage with Bon would unite each of his two beloveds to another version of Henry himself, thus sustaining his special relation to each of them rather than, like an ordinary marriage, taking them away from him. And Sutpen dreams of a plantation hierarchy as pure and, it turns out, as brittle as the hopes of Henry or Quentin.

Shreve, feeling how intensely Quentin has been drawn in to the repetitive pattern, prods him to embellish the skeleton of facts about a later incident by imagining still another repetition of Rosa's ride out to the Sutpen place to face Clytie and climb the stairs and settle something about Henry (466–67). This time, though, Clytie sets the stairs aflame so that Rosa cannot reach them. The pattern might seem to break when Clytie and Henry burn to death and Rosa dies in shock, but it lives on to repeat itself in Quentin's memory, even now as he remembers the story.

By identifying so closely with Henry at the end, Quentin caves in to the betrayal in Henry's submissive repetition of Sutpen's heartless quest. He caves in to Henry's refusal to assert a difference in will or imagination. However reluctantly, Henry repeats his father's standards and those of the social world he has grown up into, adding only the anguish that his cold father seems immune to. This matches the echo chamber Quentin of *The Sound and the Fury,* who desperately tries to hold on to what he imagines he once had, rather than grow into something different. It is partly in tune, as well, with the furious impulse to storytelling in *Absalom, Absalom!,* since storytelling is a form of repetition. But it is also deeply antithetical to *Absalom*'s feverish urge to reinvent a story not only by telling it but also by telling it again in a different way over and over, sometimes in outlandish ways that exceed anything its readers are likely to expect.

Even in the last words of the book, Quentin caves in to repetition: "*I dont. I dont! I dont hate it! I dont hate it!*" In the last paragraphs, as Shreve sharpens the focus more intensely on the South, he presses at Quentin's identification with the South. That converges with Quentin's identification with Henry, because Henry's choice to read Bon through the social lens of miscegenation-fear rather than the personal and psychological lens of incest-fear makes Henry a representative figure of the South's saddest legacy. For there, where blacks and whites came into closer and more regular contact than in the North, the daily testimony of ordinary personal relations was mostly pushed aside by the ideologically inundating system of hate that Henry succumbs to.

The turn in emphasis, then, from incest to miscegenation also turns the novel's address less to the personal and more to the social, or turns it to the personal in a different way, by exposing how we can allow the personal to be overwhelmed by the social, as Henry allows his love for his brother to be overwhelmed by social taboo.

Shreve, who knows his audience, plays sarcastically to Quentin's hysteria about miscegenation. Jocularly, he mimics the most grotesque turn-of-the-century prophets of white and Anglo-Saxon doom, because he knows that Quentin, like Henry but not like Sutpen, has enough self-doubt to feel hurt by his own horror at miscegenation. Ostensibly, Faulkner means to make fun of miscegenation-fear by satirically voicing its most extreme claims about how whites will supposedly be engulfed into blackness. One might wonder, though, if Faulkner is not on both sides, making fun of fears that he himself cannot escape, for Jim Bond seems to embody a white fantasy of the threatening black. To be sure, other blacks in the novel are not like Bond, and Faulkner covers himself with a convenient explanation, making Bond inherit his low intelligence from his dull-witted mother, whom his father has apparently sought out exactly because her hulking stupidity can confirm the white image of black inferiority that he clings to. Still, the image of Bond can trouble even those readers who recognize it as satirical. Its capacity to threaten indicates how Faulkner could play on the sensitivities of his audience. By contrast, the idiocy of a white man, such as Quentin's brother Benjy in *The Sound and the Fury,* though it can seem so threatening that his family has him gelded, strikes none of the touchy social chords that make the conception of Jim Bond threatening or offensive to readers and, as Shreve intends, to Quentin.

And so when Quentin says at the end that he does not hate the South, speaking while he comes to identify through Henry with what seems most hateful in the South, he falls into yet another self-referential and self-destructive repetition, saying, in effect, I don't hate myself, I don't hate myself. Of course he does hate himself, as would be clear from his overinsistent repetition in those concluding sentences, highlighted by italics and exclamation points, even if we did not know from

The Sound and the Fury that he goes on to kill himself. He kills himself, though, not only from hate but also from love for those desires in himself that his hate seems to threaten, and his final plea shows that his feeling for the South is just as painfully contradictory.

BEGINNING AND ENDING

Quentin in *The Sound and the Fury* kills himself so that he can never—or so he imagines—change and can only repeat. We can hear that urge to freeze time in *Absalom, Absalom!* as he repeats the Sutpen-Coldfield story to Shreve. But despite its fascinated repetition, *Absalom, Absalom!*, as we have begun to see, does not keep simply repeating. It changes, and the change breaks the cycle and turns it into conclusion.

The series of explanations for Henry's murder of Bon, the murder that propels the novel's plot, comes to a halt. The fourth and last account, the italicized "either neither" story of miscegenation, must present something of great explanatory power if it is not to leave the feeling that, after four tries, we have really made no progress but only launched an endless series in which each new explanation testifies to no more than our capacity to grasp ever more ingeniously after a past we can never recover. Granted, to some extent we can never recover any past. Certainly, many critics assume as much in talking about *Absalom, Absalom!* without making it an issue. But the irrecoverability of the past can tempt us too easily to throw up our hands as if there were no cause for preference among the assorted efforts to explain it.

And there is cause, in that *Absalom, Absalom!* ends not with one more in a random series of interchangeable alternatives, but rather at the end of a progression. It starts slowly. When the novel moves from Rosa's story "without rhyme or reason or shadow of excuse" to Mr. Compson's story about bigamy, it makes at most a small advance, if the move from no explanation to an alluringly told but implausible one can be called an advance. When it moves next from Mr. Compson's story of bigamy to Quentin's story of incest, it offers a more plausible explanation for Henry's motives, though not yet a sufficient one for the story at large, because if Sutpen told Henry in 1860 that Bon was Sutpen's son, then that still leaves unexplained the trump card that Sutpen held in abeyance until 1864. When the fourth account of Henry's motives adds an explanation for the trump card, it gives at last not just another explanation but actually a preferred explanation, so that when the novel finishes, it doesn't just come to a stop. It actually reaches, with whatever imperfections, a conclusion.

As Henry's motive for murder, the fear of miscegenation offers a preferred explanation because it matches the incidental details that need explaining, namely, that Sutpen tells General Compson that he holds in reserve a trump, something unspecified that goes beyond the claim that Bon is his son. Faulkner could just as well have had Sutpen first tell Henry and General Compson that Bon is part black and then, as his trump card, tell Henry that Bon is Sutpen's son, which would leave Henry deciding first to go along with miscegenation but finally, then, unable to abide incest. Indeed, aside from Sutpen's veiled description of his trump we have nothing but the italicized narrative to tell us it didn't happen that way. Certainly, that would make Henry's motives much more sympathetic, even if murder remains too extreme a solution. But the weight of narrative swings all in the other direction, with the revelation that Bon was Sutpen's son coming so long before the revelation that he was part black (331, 443), and with no portion of narrative ever claiming that Sutpen told Henry about Bon's black ancestry on that Christmas Eve in 1860, and none claiming that he told Henry anything but that at their encounter in 1864. That account, then, gains additional force partly just by coming last. There would be no reason to bring it up unless it went further to explain something that the story of incest leaves mysterious.

And so each new explanation in the series of four provides a more convincing fiction, and to put it that way leaves us short of claiming that any version offers or even could offer an underlying, final or extrafictional truth. But ironically, as the story grows more convincing in outline, it sometimes grows less convincing in its characters.

Although Mr. Compson cannot plausibly explain why Henry would oppose Bon's marriage to Judith or why the older, cosmopolitan Bon would go to a "little jerkwater college" (394), as Shreve calls it, he still presents a convincing portrait of the personalities he imagines, including his memorable picture of a languorous Bon. Next to that, Shreve's portraits of an oedipal Bon, his frenzied mother, and their lawyer can seem burlesque. At times, Shreve draws the lawyer as sheer caricature, with his ludicrous account books (*"Emotional val. plus 100% times nil. plus val. crop"*) and his spies who report Sutpen's actions to the minute (375–76), until later when it helps to have the lawyer ignorant of Sutpen's actions and so then Shreve no longer mentions the spies (414). Meanwhile, Shreve makes Eulalia Bon a stirring but ridiculous figure of male fantasy, the jilted woman that Quentin mistook Rosa for. And to Shreve, Eulalia is the jilted woman extraordinaire, for he reduces her to nothing beyond the memory of having been deserted and the craving for revenge. Her "busted water pipe of incomprehensible fury and fierce yearning and vindictiveness and jealous rage" (373) bursts only as testimony to the power and desirability of a husband left so unspecified that he ends up signifying men and husbands in general. At one point Shreve comes close to attributing the picture to Mr. Compson (379); it certainly sounds like a piece from Mr. Compson's misogynist routine.

The sexualized intensity of Shreve's tale sounds especially as if it has reached him through the Compsons when he takes up their habit of coloring things through oedipal fantasies. For example, he imagines that Bon contemplates marrying Judith as a means of revenge against his father (e.g., 426), which has, as well, the side effect of reducing Judith to a mere tool in a war between men. That sounds plausible enough, if only from the men's perspective, and the italicized narrative later confirms or at least reiterates it (445–46). But earlier on, Shreve raises less plausible but still Compson-style oedipal worries when he says that Bon was "not even thinking *I am looking upon my mother naked*" (383), with the denial ("not even thinking") only reinforcing the fantasy's strength.

But it is not Bon's fantasy; it is Shreve's about Bon, and so unnecessary to the story of Bon that it seems in some sense Shreve's (or Quentin's or Mr. Compson's) fantasy projected onto Bon. It sometimes comes as a shock for readers to recall that none of Shreve's story tells anything about Bon per se. Shreve, aided apparently by Mr. Compson and Quentin, makes it up. Almost all Bon's erratically evolving thoughts about what he might do, even his suspicion and later certainty that Sutpen is his father or that he is part black, come from Shreve until the italicized narrative finally presents one other corroboration. Though it comes from no identifiable character or perspective, that corroboration takes the narrative beyond Quentin's remark that "nobody ever did know if Bon knew that Sutpen was his father or not" (335). To be sure, Shreve presents some reasonable possibilities for Bon, suggesting, for example, that he goes to the University of Mississippi to find his father. Still, nothing impels Shreve to embellish that possibility with the wild story of the lawyer, since Bon could just as well go to Mississippi at his own direction, or his mother's, or that of anyone who knows his past and can influence his plans. But mostly Shreve's story of Bon tells, however obliquely, about the people who make it up, about the Compsons and Shreve.

And so as the explanations of Henry's motive for murder turn more reliable, the details that fill them out ironically turn more far-fetched. The inverse relation curiously makes for a kind of emotional equivalence among the several explanations, so that even as we discard the explanatory power of Mr. Compson's story of languorous New Orleans concubinage, it loses none of its imaginative power. Imaginative power is much of what finally lies at issue here as we sort out the various explanations, since even the underlying tale they compete to explain is, after all, no less a fiction than the stories that claim to explain it.

The fourth explanation sounds still less reasonable than Shreve's overwrought tale of oedipal confusion and incest. But that is the point. No one attributes the actions of Thomas and Henry Sutpen to reason. And the fourth explanation snaps Quentin out of the incest fascination he has needlessly sustained for so long before shifting the burden of explanation to race relations. That breaks the repetition that in *The Sound and the Fury* Quentin imagines he can lock himself into forever through an endlessly peaceful and dreamy death.

The discovery that Bon was part black thus repeats yet again the process of explaining the story, but changes that process as well. Like the wistaria blooming for the second time that summer, and like Rosa who associates herself with the wistaria, it breaks the pattern. By driving to the Sutpen house with Quentin, by punching out Clytie beneath the stairs (438, 460), and by returning to the Sutpen house with medical aid for Henry, Rosa—as Shreve puts it—"refused at the last to be a ghost" (451). She breaks the pattern she has been locked into, the 44-year paralysis of repetition in memory. To be sure, even the changes partake of repetition, since Rosa, as she breaks her paralysis, does so by riding out again, even twice more, to the Sutpen house for a confrontation with Clytie and Henry. But these last two times no one summons her to go, as before she was summoned by Wash Jones (presumably on Judith's or even Henry's errand), or summoned into her engagement by Sutpen as in a *"ukase, a decree"* (205). On the contrary, here at the end Rosa inverts the pattern; she summons others to go with her. So that at the end, Quentin's and Rosa's and the novel's furious repetition spills over into a willfulness that cannot be contained, a repetition that is no longer so repetitive, at once bounded and breaking its bounds, closing and opening, making an end to the novel by grafting onto it a beginning of something that goes beyond its own recirculation of generation trying impossibly to repeat generation, until repetition and change can be neither denied nor distinguished one from the other, "compounded each of both yet either neither."

Appendix:
The Narrative Structure of
Absalom, Absalom!

CHAPTER 1 (3–33)

Time present: a little after 2 P.M. until almost sundown on a September day in 1909, with brief glances forward to later that evening (9, 10–11)

Time past: June 1833 to 1866 (9)

Perspective: authorial or external narrator, though within that mostly through Rosa

CHAPTER 2 (34–69)

Time present: twilight after supper at the Compsons (34)

Time past: June 1833–June 1838 (34, 56)

Perspective: first a nonomniscient external narrator telling what the town or Grandfather Compson knew and modulating (39–40) into the satirical voice of legend; then (49) Mr. Compson

CHAPTER 3 (70–107)

Time present: continued

Time past: mainly 1855–66, with some attention to 1833–55, and glances (98, 99) as far forward as 1869

Perspective: Mr. Compson continued, but without quotation marks and with a few italicized interjections from the external narrator

CHAPTER 4 (108–65)

Time present: continued

Time past: fall semester 1860 to when Wash comes to tell Rosa about Henry and Bon in 1865

Perspective: introduced by authorial or external narrator focused through

Quentin; then changes to Mr. Compson, with external narrator returning briefly on 159, 160, and 163

CHAPTER 5 (166–216)

Time present: Chapter 5 falls chronologically between chapters 1 and 2 (2, 3, and 4 are consecutive), as we can tell because the sun is out in chapter 5 (178) but almost down at the beginning of chapter 4 (108). In chapter 6 (218–21) we learn that when Quentin went from his father back to Rosa they didn't sit and talk, as in chapter 5, but drove out to the Sutpen place. Chapter 5 therefore concludes a little after 5 P.M. (9).

Time past: from the moment where the last chapter left off in 1865 to seven months later when Sutpen returns home (197), three months after that when he becomes engaged to Rosa (197), and two months after that when he insults her and she leaves (212)—a total of 12 months—plus some recollections of Rosa's adolescence (178–85)

Perspective: Rosa, in italics that seem "free of the limitations and restrictions of speech and hearing" (172) until p. 215, where the external narrator gives Quentin's thoughts and then gives dialogue between Quentin and Rosa

CHAPTER 6 (217–70)

Time present: ca. 12 January 1910 (217)

Time past: January 1910 and irregularly from Sutpen's insulting Rosa in 1866 to some incomplete talk about Quentin and Rosa going to the Sutpen place in September 1909

Perspective: begins authorially or externally; then Quentin's thoughts; then conversation with Shreve; then Shreve; then Quentin thinking (227–34) an italicized version of what he apparently tells Shreve; then, in one overarching parenthesis (234–70):

a) an authorial or external rendering of Quentin recalling (234–66)—at Shreve's prompting (234)—a day with Mr. Compson and (from 236) what Mr. Compson said that day, which

b) is interrupted by Quentin thinking during the time present without italics (237–38) and later—while in the background Shreve apparently talks on *"like Father"* (260, 264)—in italics again (243, 259–61, 263 [*"Yes . . . Too much, too long"*], 264), and followed by

c) either Mr. Compson (beginning at *"Beautiful lives . . ."*) or, given the italics, Quentin's memory of Mr. Compson (264–66) and by

d) Shreve talking in italics or Quentin thinking and addressing himself in the second person (266–69)

finally (269)—without italics—Shreve

Appendix

CHAPTER 7 (271–365)

Time present: continued, ca. 11 P.M. (318, 343)

Time past: from Sutpen's childhood to his death and Jones's death (in 1869)

Perspective: authorial or external (except for one italicized switch to Mr. Compson, 346–49), but mostly through Quentin (with interruptions from Shreve), Quentin's memory of his father's or grandfather's telling (and in one case his grandmother's, 350), of his father's retelling of Grandfather's telling, and of his father's retelling of Grandfather's retelling of Sutpen's telling

CHAPTER 8 (366–448)

Time present: continued, ca. midnight (366, 379, 405)

Time past: from Christmas Eve 1860 back to and through Bon's childhood, through the night in 1864 when Sutpen tells Henry about Bon's mother and the day when Henry kills Bon, with some glances ahead to the night when Quentin goes to the old Sutpen place with Rosa

Perspective: first a nonomniscient and perhaps here and there satirical external narrator, then mostly Shreve, which is as if it were Quentin, and sometimes—in italics without quotation marks—as if it were Shreve and Quentin both, or even "Charles-Shreve and Quentin-Henry" "compounded each of both yet either neither" (417, 439)

CHAPTER 9 (449–71)

Time present: continued, ca. 1 A.M. (466)

Time past: the September evening in 1909 and a December day in 1909

Perspective: external, largely through Quentin's thoughts and memories, including memories that Shreve seems privy to

Notes and References

Chapter 3

1. First-time readers will do best not to look ahead to the Chronology and Genealogy, which give away much of the plot. Faulkner put them at the end, though other novelists sometimes put such materials at the beginning. For further discussion of differences between the 1936 version of the Chronology and Genealogy and the rest of the novel, see Robert Dale Parker, "The Chronology and Genealogy of *Absalom, Absalom!*: The Authority of Fiction and the Fiction of Authority," *Studies in American Fiction* 14 (1986): 191–98.

Chapter 4

1. *Selected Letters of William Faulkner*, ed. Joseph Blotner (New York: Random House, 1977), 44–45.

2. *Faulkner's Revision of "Absalom, Absalom!": A Collation of the Manuscript and the Published Book*, ed. Gerald Langford (Austin: University of Texas Press, 1971), 73–79.

3. William Faulkner, *The Sound and the Fury* (1929; reprint, New York: Random House, n.d.), 410.

Chapter 5

1. Again and again through the novel, Faulkner refers to the missing piece or pieces by the vague word "something," which allows him to point to what's missing without identifying it, thus intensifying the suspense. See Robert Dale Parker, *Faulkner and the Novelistic Imagination* (Urbana: University of Illinois Press, 1985).

2. William Faulkner, *Light in August* (1932; reprint, New York: Vintage, 1987), 126.

3. See especially Lyle Saxon, *Fabulous New Orleans* (New York: Century, 1928), 177–201 and passim; David Paul Ragan calls attention to a passage from this book in *William Faulkner's "Absalom, Absalom!": A Critical Study* (Ann Arbor, Mich.: UMI Research Press, 1987), 187.

4. Langford, 110.

5. The photograph figures more prominently in "Evangeline," an early story that Faulkner later revised into *Absalom, Absalom!* In the story, it does indeed depict Bon's New Orleans wife. See *Uncollected Stories of William Faulkner,* ed. Joseph Blotner (New York: Random House, 1979).

6. Children were burned in sacrifice to Moloch, an Ammonite god best known from 2 Kings 23.10 and as one of the more celebrated residents of Milton's Hell in *Paradise Lost* I, ll. 392–405.

7. William Faulkner, *Sanctuary* (1931; reprint, New York: Vintage, 1987), 227–28, 231.

Chapter 6

1. Langford, 272–73. Cleanth Brooks first called attention to these additions to the manuscript in *William Faulkner: The Yoknapatawpha Country* (New Haven, Conn.: Yale University Press, 1963), 437–38.

2. For similar sidelong references to Quentin's and Rosa's evening at the Sutpen house and to Quentin gaining crucial information there, see pp. 227 and 342, which, like the passage on p. 332, Faulkner added after finishing the manuscript (Langford, 190, 278).

3. Perhaps out of carelessness or from sheer pleasure in teasing complications, Faulkner throws some readers off by referring once to Jim Bond as "Charles Bon's son" (269), meaning Charles [Etienne Saint-Valery] Bon's son, the grandson of the character usually referred to as Charles Bon.

4. The parenthesis, restored in the 1986 edition, runs from p. 234 to p. 270 (see the appendix). My students often show a bemused fascination with the close parenthesis, readily noticeable because it falls at the end of the chapter, but too far from its open parenthesis to connect the two. It has a peculiar editorial history, one that can represent the difficulties of establishing final textual authority for *Absalom, Absalom!* or many other books. The manuscript, typescript, and 1936 and 1986 editions all give different versions of where to put the parenthesis. Noel Polk, editor of the 1986 edition, has apparently picked what he believes Faulkner would have chosen if Faulkner had seen all the variants. Polk does not explain his evidence or reasoning, and though I have no quarrel with his decision here or elsewhere, let us underline that it is a decision, based (one supposes, after comparing the consistent

manuscript parenthesis and the inconsistent typescript parenthesis) on a principle of sustaining logical consistency in a novel that often defies logic and on a manuscript variant in a passage that Faulkner later restructured. To accept Polk's decision, we must reject Faulkner's later revision of the parenthesis as an error. This makes a thorny example of the ways the 1986 text is editorially constructed rather than a pure representation of Faulkner's so-called final intent, which seems not to have been so final after all.

5. In *The Sound and the Fury*, Luster is too young in 1928 to have been born when Quentin goes hunting in *Absalom, Absalom!*, some time before 1909. Indeed, in *The Sound and the Fury* Quentin hunts with Luster's uncle, Versh. In the typescript, Faulkner crossed out the character's earlier name, "Dan," and changed it to "Luster," thus referring to *The Sound and the Fury* in a way that comically establishes difference as well as continuity. That could be a careless slip, but might not be, since the mere reference to Luster in the first part of *The Sound and the Fury* often marks which time or year the narrative refers to.

6. For a study of Faulkner's youthful infatuation with turn-of-the-century aestheticism, with reproductions of drawings by Beardsley and by Faulkner, see Lothar Hönnighausen, *William Faulkner: The Art of Stylization in His Early Graphic and Literary Work* (Cambridge: Cambridge University Press, 1987).

7. Faulkner, *Light in August*, 130; see also 13, 14, 193.

Chapter 7

1. See especially the classic study by C. Vann Woodward, *The Strange Career of Jim Crow*, 3rd ed. (New York: Oxford University Press, 1974).

2. Langford, 11; Elisabeth Muhlenfeld, Introduction to *William Faulkner's "Absalom, Absalom!": A Critical Casebook*, ed. Muhlenfeld (New York: Garland, 1984), xxvii, xxxi.

3. For a more detailed study of this passage, see Parker, *Faulkner and the Novelistic Imagination*, 139–42. In returning to nearly the same materials, I now make the point about Henry less confidently and take more interest in Faulkner's concern to undermine confidence.

Selected Bibliography

Primary Works

Collected Stories. New York: Random House, 1950. Includes two Quentin stories, "That Evening Sun" and "A Justice," and a Sutpen story, "Wash," rewritten for chapter 7 of *Absalom*.

The Sound and the Fury. Edited by Noel Polk. New York: Vintage, 1987.

Uncollected Stories of William Faulkner. Edited by Joseph Blotner. New York: Random House, 1979. Includes "Evangeline," an early version of the novel.

Faulkner's Revision of "Absalom, Absalom!": A Collation of the Manuscript and the Published Book. Edited by Gerald Langford. Austin: University of Texas Press, 1971. Useful, though it must be consulted with caution, because the editing is unreliable.

William Faulkner Manuscripts, 13. "Absalom, Absalom!": Typescript Setting Copy and Miscellaneous Material. Edited by Noel Polk. New York: Garland, 1987.

Selected Letters of William Faulkner. Edited by Joseph Blotner. New York: Random House, 1977.

Faulkner in the University: Class Conferences at the University of Virginia, 1957–58. Edited by Frederick L. Gwynn and Joseph L. Blotner. Charlottesville: University of Virginia Press, 1959. Faulkner's comments years later, when his view of his own work sometimes seems less convincing.

Secondary Works

Books

Blotner, Joseph. *Faulkner: A Biography*. 2 vols. New York: Random House, 1974.

————. *Faulkner: A Biography*. One-volume edition. New York: Random House, 1984. The two, differing versions of Blotner's biography are each indispensable.

Brooks, Cleanth. *William Faulkner: The Yoknapatawpha Country*. New Haven, Conn.: Yale University Press, 1963. Brooks has fallen out of fashion among some more theoretical critics, but this remains a classic study.

————. *William Faulkner: Toward Yoknapatawpha and Beyond*. New Haven, Conn.: Yale University Press, 1978. Sutpen, Rosa Coldfield, and narrative structure.

Davis, Thadious M. *Faulkner's "Negro": Art and the Southern Context*. Baton Rouge: Louisiana State University Press, 1983. "Negro" as character and concept.

Guerard, Albert J. *The Triumph of the Novel: Dickens, Dostoevsky, Faulkner*. New York: Oxford University Press, 1976. *Absalom* as the "culminating novel of Conradian impressionism." Seasoned and thought-provoking.

Hunt, John W. *William Faulkner: Art in Theological Tension*. Syracuse, N.Y.: Syracuse University Press, 1965. Dated, but a thoughtful study, more philosophical than theological.

Irwin, John T. *Doubling and Incest/Repetition and Revenge: A Speculative Reading of Faulkner*. Baltimore: Johns Hopkins University Press, 1975. Assumes that *The Sound and the Fury* and *Absalom, Absalom!* are one text and reads them together psychoanalytically, focusing on Quentin and Bon. A major study, perhaps the most interesting book on Faulkner, though marred by an unquestioning reliance on classically psychoanalytic assumptions of male centrality that seem dated now even to many psychoanalytically oriented critics. Also treats the characters as if they had the full histories and psychological depth of people and treats the characters' speculations as facts.

Kartiganer, Donald M. *The Fragile Thread: The Meaning of Form in Faulkner's Novels*. Amherst: University of Massachusetts Press, 1979. Especially insightful on Mr. Compson.

Kinney, Arthur F. *Faulkner's Narrative Poetics: Style as Vision*. Amherst: University of Massachusetts Press, 1978. Especially shrewd on Rosa and Mr. Compson.

Matthews, John T. *The Play of Faulkner's Language*. Ithaca, N.Y.: Cornell University Press, 1982. This study, influenced by Jacques Derrida, gives its best chapter to *Absalom*.

Millgate, Michael. *The Achievement of William Faulkner*. New York: Random House, 1966. The first broad study of Faulkner to make extensive use of manuscript research.

Minter, David. *William Faulkner: His Life and Work*. Baltimore: Johns Hopkins University Press, 1980. Especially useful on the first half or so of Faulkner's life.

Montauzon, Christine de. *Faulkner's "Absalom, Absalom!" and Interpretability: The Inexplicable Unseen.* Berne, Switzerland: Peter Lang, 1985. A little known theoretical study of the novel's resistance to interpretation.

Muhlenfeld, Elisabeth, ed. *William Faulkner's "Absalom, Absalom!": A Critical Casebook.* New York: Garland, 1984. Valuable collection of essays. Muhlenfeld's well-researched and thorough introduction contains the fullest treatment of the novel's composition, with reasonable though unprovable speculations about what prompted Faulkner's imagination. Perhaps some promptings lay further from his immediate experience during the months he wrote the novel than Muhlenfeld assumes.

Parker, Robert Dale. *Faulkner and the Novelistic Imagination.* Urbana: University of Illinois Press, 1985. Focuses on narrative structure and character, only modestly overlapping with the present book.

Porter, Carolyn. *Seeing and Being: The Plight of the Participant Observer in Emerson, James, Adams, and Faulkner.* Middletown, Conn.: Wesleyan University Press, 1981. A patient, thoughtful discussion of the novel and its social and historical world.

Ragan, David Paul. *William Faulkner's "Absalom, Absalom!": A Critical Study.* Ann Arbor, Mich.: UMI Research Press, 1987. A detailed study based on wide reading in Faulkner scholarship. Much plot summary with little methodological reflection. More sympathetic with Sutpen and less sympathetic with Rosa Coldfield than the present study.

Ross, Stephen M. *Fiction's Inexhaustible Voice: Speech and Writing in Faulkner.* Athens: University of Georgia Press, 1989. An excellent book that includes a discussion of the novel's dialogue between singular and multiple voices. Highly recommended.

Schoenberg, Estella. *Old Tales and Talking: Quentin Compson in William Faulkner's "Absalom, Absalom!" and Related Works.* Jackson: University Press of Mississippi, 1977. Poorly thought through study of intriguingly selected materials.

Sundquist, Eric J. *Faulkner: The House Divided.* Baltimore: Johns Hopkins University Press, 1983. The historical context of attitudes towards miscegenation.

Taylor, Walter. *Faulkner's Search for a South.* Urbana: University of Illinois Press, 1983. *Absalom*'s revision of racist stereotypes, especially the tragic mulatto.

Waggoner, Hyatt H. *William Faulkner: From Jefferson to the World.* Lexington: University of Kentucky Press, 1959. Path-breaking early study, dated but still interesting.

Weinstein, Arnold L. *Vision and Response in Modern Fiction*. Ithaca, N.Y.: Cornell University Press, 1974. The role of feelings and emotions.

Articles

Brodsky, Claudia. "The Working of Narrative in *Absalom, Absalom!*" *Amerikastudien* 23 (1978): 240–59. Dry but alertly observed, rigorous study of the novel's narrative methods.

Hagan, John. "*Déjà Vu* and the Effect of Timelessness in Faulkner's *Absalom, Absalom!*" *Bucknell Review* 11 (March 1963): 31–52. Excellent observation of repeated patterns; less convincing in interpreting them.

———. "Fact and Fancy in *Absalom, Absalom!*" *College English* 24 (1962): 215–18. Sensible review of how Quentin learns that Bon is part black.

Hagopian, John V. "Black Insight in *Absalom, Absalom!*" *Faulkner Studies* 1 (1980): 29–37. Quentin learns that Bon is part black by looking at Clytie.

Krause, David. "Opening Pandora's Box: Re-Reading Compson's Letter and Faulkner's *Absalom, Absalom!*" *Centennial Review* 30 (1986): 358–82. A series of insightful, intelligent articles based on poststructuralist theory, perhaps sometimes too cleverly. Highly recommended.

———. "Reading Bon's Letter and Faulkner's *Absalom, Absalom!*" *PMLA* 99 (1984): 225–41.

———. "Reading Shreve's Letters and Faulkner's *Absalom, Absalom!*" *Studies in American Fiction* 11 (Autumn 1983): 153–69.

Parr, Susan Resneck. "The Fourteenth Image of the Blackbird: Another Look at Truth in *Absalom, Absalom!*" *Arizona Quarterly* 35 (1979): 153–64. Quentin's belief that Bon is part black is conjectured or intuited.

Price, Steve. "Shreve's Bon in *Absalom, Absalom!*" *Mississippi Quarterly* 39 (Summer 1986): 325–35. Good review of matters most critics overlook. Unquestioningly assumes that the italicized episode in chapter 8 comes through Shreve's perspective.

Schmidtberger, Loren F. "*Absalom, Absalom!*: What Clytie Knew." *Mississippi Quarterly* 35 (Summer 1982): 255–63. Good observations; perhaps turns overly speculative.

Zoellner, Robert H. "Faulkner's Prose Style in *Absalom, Absalom!*" *American Literature* 30 (January 1959): 486–502.

Index

The Author

Robert Dale Parker teaches at the University of Illinois at Urbana-Champaign. He is also the author of *Faulkner and the Novelistic Imagination* (1985) and *The Unbeliever: The Poetry of Elizabeth Bishop* (1988).